Its Head Came Off
by Accident

Its Head Came Off by Accident

A Memoir

A Memoir

Muffy Mead-Ferro

TWODOT®

GUILFORD, CONNECTICUT
HELENA, MONTANA
AN IMPRINT OF GLOBE PEQUOT PRESS

For my father

To buy books in quantity for corporate use
or incentives, call **(800) 962-0973**
or e-mail **premiums@GlobePequot.com**.

A · TWODOT® · BOOK

TwoDot is an imprint of Globe Pequot Press.

Project editor: David Legere
Text design: Sheryl P. Kober
Layout: Justin Marciano

Library of Congress Cataloging-in-Publication Data is available on file.

ISBN 978-0-7627-8064-8

Printed in the United States of America

10 9 8 7 6 5 4 3 2 1

Contents

Preface vii

1 Alfalfa 1

2 The Lower Ranch, Pete and Mary 12

3 Sylvia and P.C., Cliff and Martha 28

4 Houses, Barns, and a Hole in the Ground 43

5 The Men 58

6 Wrecks and Near-Wrecks 74

7 The Martins 82

8 Real Work and a New Horse 99

9 Riding Up from the Drag 112

10 A Fissure in the Landscape 126

11 Little Joe 137

12 A Slow Dissolve 150

13 Back to the Pig Farm, and to Mormon Row 156

Afterword 171

Acknowledgments 175

About the Author 176

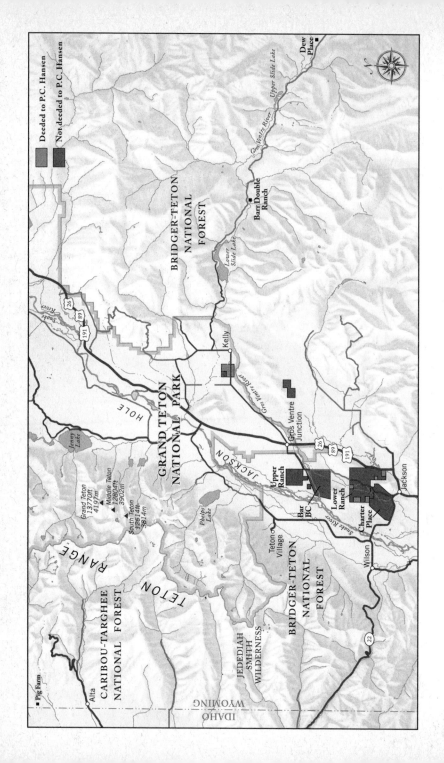

Preface

"DON'T HAVE CHICKENS," MY MOTHER SAID TO ME ONE DAY, BUT SHE didn't go to the trouble of adding why not to. That was like her—to make a pronouncement I'd presumably be expected to remember and follow even if I had no idea how it could be relevant, given that I was perhaps eight years old at the time, and fowl were not on my wish list, but I still remember wondering what it was she didn't like about them. They were noisy . . . dirty . . . mean—what? My mother never said. Not elaborating was typical of her, and so a general lack of background information about things my mother held as truths was a key feature of my childhood, growing up on a cattle ranch in the northwest corner of Wyoming.

But then, not asking for background information was a key feature of my own personality, so the pros and cons of chickens weren't the only things I was not too clear on. My hope was that by not making inquiries I would somehow appear inherently knowledgeable (or at least, not appear inherently ignorant), so I wasn't in the habit of asking my mother why we made the decisions we did when it came to livestock—chickens, cattle, horses—or just about anything else. To ask why, I feared, might have elicited the question, "Why do you think?" since my mother really seemed to enjoy having my brothers and me figure things out for ourselves. And to that I was afraid I'd have a wrong answer so I simply, most of the time, did as she said. And then on a more frequent basis, as the years went by, did not do as she said, but in either case without usually knowing the why behind her ways. She wasn't big on volunteering explanations for things, and I wasn't big on requesting them. I preferred to remain secretly bewildered, and just keep my fingers crossed that things would eventually come to me.

What might be wrong with chickens never did come to me, but my mother's comment on them stuck, and I noticed, after she died, that some of her pronouncements carried even more weight with me than when she was still with us. Not only could I not seem to get out from under my mother's words, but my unasked questions could never be answered.

"Cats are a nuisance." In what way? And does this make dogs a nuisance, too, or just cats?

"Wyoming girls don't have umbrellas." Not ever? Or only when we're in Wyoming? What if we've gone out without a hat?

"You always undo the back cinch first." But how could that make any difference when I'm going to undo both of them?

"Don't have chickens." Fine; as an eight-year-old, I wasn't planning on it.

But then chickens became a possibility for me a number of years after my mother died, when my husband Michael and I, along with our two children, Belle and Joe, came into possession of our own Wyoming agricultural property: an old pig farm on the very western edge of the state. The place has plenty of room for a chicken coop, and some of the neighbors have chickens and seem to get along fine with them. I've wondered if we would enjoy tending the hens and having fresh eggs, but we haven't gotten them. For all I know about myself, it's because Mary said not to.

I did call my mother Mary, and I called my father Pete. I can't remember when we started using their first names, but I once heard someone else ask my mother why we called them Mary and Pete, in a way that suggested they might be more interested in why my parents allowed it than why we did it. Mary's explanation was that we were just following the example of the hands who lived with us on the ranch. She didn't go on to say whether that was for good or for bad, but the way I took it was that it was for good, because I didn't think I'd go too far wrong if I did what the ranch hands did. That they were not only my elders but my betters was a fact of ranch life I did pick up on without help.

When I've thought of the Wyoming cattle ranch I was raised on, the variety of people who worked there, and the importance the operation had to so many of them—and to me—I've had to wonder how Mary, if she were still alive, might have regarded our little pig farm.

But I almost hate to ask myself that question. It's not a cattle ranch. It's not even a pig farm. When my husband Michael and I first bought it we found, in the dirt-coated detritus of the cinder-block pig barn, that the animal vaccination records didn't go beyond the late 1970s. The neighbors to the south, Lorin and Liza Wilson, recollected that the hog operation had been abandoned sometime shortly after that, more than thirty years ago, and we weren't planning on resurrecting it.

We ended up calling our property "the Pig Farm" anyway, because everyone else in the surrounding community of Alta, Wyoming, called it that and we gave up trying to explain where our place was by other means. You could tell people it was that property on the corner of State Line and Kaufmann Road. You could tell them it was the farm just north of Wilsons'. But whatever you told them that would finally locate the property in their minds, they'd still say, "Oh—the Pig Farm."

I'd wanted to call it the M Lazy M, myself, after we took possession of the place, because that is Michael's and my livestock brand. Mary and Pete had come up with the M Lazy M brand for themselves when they bought their first cows back in the 1950s, and to mark the occasion Pete had an engraved silver buckle made for Mary, with the M LAZY M embossed in gold. Pete held on to the M Lazy M brand from then on, even though it went out of use, and stayed out of use for decades. Of course, ranches themselves often go by the name of the brand that's used on the cattle, and the brand will change hands when the land does, as a part of the property. But sometimes a brand will stay with an individual and go where he or she goes. Most of my ancestors have had a habit of holding on to their brands, as a separate asset.

The Double T and the X Diamond—brands that had been in our family a long time, and had been seared onto the hides of many thousands of cattle—had been given to my brothers, Brad and Matt, respectively, to use on their own places. And my father had said, once we bought the Pig Farm, that he wanted to give the M Lazy M brand to me. It was a good brand, too; not as good as the Double T or the X Diamond, but a good brand.

Mary explained to me when I was little what was so desirable about both the Double T and the X Diamond, and this also illustrates what gives the M Lazy M slightly less utility. As I said, it was not my mother's habit to volunteer much in the way of background information, but I'd made a remark one day that did call for her to inform me of some basic facts. With all the wisdom of a grade-schooler I'd questioned the worth of the Double T.

"I don't see why our brand is a Double T," I said. Then, obliged to point out the obvious, I added, "It doesn't stand for anything." Our family name started with M, and my grandparents' name was Hansen. Who was T? No one.

My mother did not stoop to replying with, "I'm aware that our name does not start with T." Instead she said, "That's not what matters." She said the value of the Double T and the X Diamond came down to the fact that they were graphically simple and that they were old, two attributes which typically went hand in hand. With 20,000-some brands in the state of Wyoming it became more and more difficult to come up with a simple one—easy to brand and easy to read—that hadn't already been thought of, or wasn't too close to one that had. The idea being, if your neighbor's brand was an X, you couldn't register a brand that was an X Bar in the same location on the animal, because it would make it too easy to rustle their herd.

I could see the beauty and the logic of what Mary was saying, even back then. I loved her explanation, in fact, and unbeknownst to her I think I repeated that information about cattle brands to quite a few people who may or may not have been interested. And more than thirty years later, when we needed a brand for the Pig Farm, I was glad to finally inherit a family brand and not have to try and come up with one from scratch—particularly when it just so happened (not that it was what mattered) that both my husband's and my first names started with M.

I already had my mother's M Lazy M belt buckle, the one that Pete had had made for her more than fifty years earlier. It was the single item he'd told me specifically to make sure and find, after she died, because he didn't want it to get lost in the confusion that followed her accident. I'd looked for it in her closet and dresser drawers and finally found it put away in a plastic fishing-tackle box where she'd kept some earrings sorted into pairs.

But while I'd easily gotten the historic buckle in hand, the transfer of the brand itself was not quite so glitch-free.

Pete called the Wyoming Livestock Board in Cheyenne to let them know he wanted to change the brand's ownership. While he waited on the phone they checked their records, and when they picked up the line again, they informed him that he didn't own any brand called the M Lazy M. He objected; he was pretty sure he did own an M Lazy M, having come up with it in the 1950s, and having paid the recording fees ever since.

No, the clerk told him, there's no M Lazy M brand here; however, he *did* own an M Lazy W. She wondered if maybe that's what he was talking about. At that moment, after all those decades, Pete realized his and Mary's mistake. They'd turned the second M clockwise when a lazy letter was supposed to fall back, and right then the M had become a lazy W, and it still was one.

"You've got to be kidding," is what I believe I said, when that phone conversation was related to me. A long-standing family legacy—a brand that had finally been passed down to me where I stood at the end of the line with a pig farm in hand—a mistake? I didn't want to seem ungrateful, but that hit me rather flat.

Had Mary lived long enough to be informed of that error, however, my guess is she would have laughed about it, and that's what Pete did when he told me I was the new owner of a brand I'd never heard of until that day: the M Lazy W. I didn't laugh, though. *Let things be called what they've always been called,* I thought, and decided to move forward as if I were ignorant of the Livestock Board's revelation. Not only have I continued to refer to the hand-me-down brand as the M Lazy M, but I had a big sign made, to hang from the pole gate at the Pig Farm, spelling out M LAZY M for everyone, coming and going, to see.

As a property name, however, it has never caught on. Everyone around there, the Wilsons, the Kaufmanns, and everyone else, continues to refer to our property as the Pig Farm—*Let things be called what they've always been called,* I guess is their thinking—and as a matter of convenience, we've followed suit.

Of course, even if it were known as the M Lazy M, that wouldn't turn our place into a legitimate cattle ranch. At 125 acres it's a postage stamp as far as Wyoming ranches go. More important, it has no open water. When we bought the property it did have adequate water rights, ones that were established back in the 1800s, but the irrigation water came down not through an open, running stream but through a buried, cast-iron pipe to which you attach sprinkler lines at intermittent risers. When we first bought the place, I had no clue as to how this procedure was done. And unlike the ranch I grew up on, there weren't any trees. They had been cleared out a hundred years ago by homesteaders intent on plowing, so there was no natural shelter for cows, horses, or anyone else. When we bought the property, it was not fenced, not even the perimeter, and obviously not the separate pastures we would need to efficiently manage a herd of cattle.

The Pig Farm was also located, from my family's perspective, on the wrong side of the Tetons, near the very small town of Alta. The right side of the Tetons would mean Jackson Hole, the seat of our family history. Not that I thought there was anything great about Jackson when I was growing up, but at least it was a legitimate town. Alta is so small it doesn't merit a pin dot on most maps of Wyoming, and it doesn't even have its own post office.

I wouldn't have looked for land in Alta in the first place except for the fact that Pete and my stepmom Leslie live there. Pete and Les had moved from Jackson Hole to Alta about ten years before we started looking for agricultural property, and I had driven past the place we would eventually own on the way to their house many times. I did like the view of the mountains, though it was disorienting to look up at the Grand Teton and see the North Face dropping off at the left of the peak instead of the right.

What seemed more peculiar to me when Michael and I started looking seriously at land around that tiny community was not the aspect of the Grand itself, but the terrain beneath it. Geologic forces on the west side of the Tetons, so I was told in high school, had been very different than on the east. The emergence of the Teton Mountains had been almost like a trapdoor opening—a quick (geologically speaking) and colossal upthrust of rock which fell away dramatically to the level valley floor on the east. The community of Alta was situated on the trapdoor, and rather than having been graded flat by the glacier sailing past on the east side of the fault, it was pushed into wrinkles by the forces of the upward thrust.

As I would drive up State Line Road looking for property, two wheels in the dirt of Idaho and two in the dirt of Wyoming, I marveled at the up-down, up-down nature of the landscape and wondered if I could get used to it. It was hard to picture following cattle up the little hills and then down the little hills, and it began to dawn on me that irrigating would be a completely different matter on that wavy ground.

The nearly 14,000-foot summit of the Grand Teton was not the only element dividing Jackson and Alta, however. In fact, I had some opinions against Alta and the whole area that were both deep-seated and quite shallow. Even though I didn't think growing up in Jackson Hole on the east side of the Tetons was particularly special at the time, I still managed to look down on that barely there community on the other side of the mountains, and I'm pretty sure my brothers Brad and Matt did too. This was mostly because Alta is perilously close to the Idaho state line, and we didn't feel that our neighbor to the west was all that good of a state. Idaho, as far as we knew, was known for potatoes—it even said so on their license plate, FAMOUS POTATOES—while the Wyoming license plate depicted a bucking horse and rider, as it had ever since the 1930s.

(I never knew who the rider was—some say Stub Farlow, some say Clayton Danks, both legendary bronc riders in their time—but I heard the horse was supposed to be Steamboat, a black horse born in Wyoming who unseated almost everyone who tried to ride him during his rodeo career in the early 1900s. Steamboat was supposedly named because his snorting was so loud it resembled the blow of a steamboat whistle, as if his twisting jumps and stiff landings weren't enough to rattle a would-be rider. He was inducted into the Pro Rodeo Hall of Fame in 1979, and people still talk about the horse—at least in Wyoming.)

Just comparing the two states of Idaho and Wyoming by how they summed themselves up on their own license plates might help to illustrate how my brothers and I came by our opinions. It's true that we should not have thought of the town of Alta itself as part of Idaho, because it isn't. But if you live in Alta, Wyoming, you attend school, buy groceries, and get your mail and everything else five miles away in Driggs, Idaho, because it's much easier to cross the imaginary frontier of the state line than it is to cross the very real barrier of the Tetons. So from a practical standpoint Alta residents are more a part of Idaho than Wyoming, in more with the potato farmers than the cattle ranchers.

Despite all of this, the Pig Farm was the best place my husband Michael and I could find. It was agricultural land, surrounded by agricultural land (owned mainly by the Wilsons and the Kaufmanns, whose families had farmed there for more than a century). It was right down the road from Pete, and it was, if only by the breadth of a thin black line on a US map, in Wyoming. Having a place in Wyoming was what I cared most about; having a place in Wyoming, to replace the one I'd lost.

Well, not so much "lost." More like sold.

Out of practical necessity, yet with many regrets, Brad and Matt and I sold the portion of the family ranch that had been owned by my mother, known as the Bar B C, eight years after she died in an accident. For one thing, we had to pay inheritance taxes, and for another, we couldn't envision how to own the ranch jointly—not in the long run, as the generations fanned out in our wake. So we sold it and all three of us wanted to turn the proceeds, derived though they were from a family tragedy, into ranches of our own.

We were each in our forties by the time the sale closed and coming back to ranching belatedly. Matt and Brad had both been educated as lawyers, and it was their law careers, not ranching, that had kept a roof over their heads. But it was to a great extent the early Wyoming ranchers who shaped the state, both from a political and an economic standpoint, and the law business and its close relative, politics, had kept company with ranching in our family from the beginning.

My great-grandfather, who started the ranch I grew up on, had also been instrumental in the formation of Teton County, Wyoming, and was one of its first commissioners. Later he served as a member of the Wyoming House of Representatives. His son, my mother's father, whom I called Granddad, had been elected Wyoming's governor (WYOMING'S NEW COWBOY GOVERNOR, said the *Salt Lake Tribune* at the time), and then a US senator. My mother had taken leave of the ranch to run for governor herself, though unsuccessfully. And my younger brother Matt ran for governor of Wyoming and actually did get elected. (I don't mean to sound surprised, because I agreed with my grandmother, whose remark, upon being informed of Matt's victory, was, "I really can't think of anybody who'd be better.")

So there'd been a long-standing connection between cattle ranching and government in Wyoming, particularly in the Hansen-Mead family.

I would not maintain this connection with my own career, as I pulled out of law school two weeks before I was due to start with the realization that I wanted to be a writer, not a lawyer, though I ended up on what is possibly the lowest rung of that particular ladder, as a copywriter in advertising. But despite our different career choices and some of the practical decisions we each had to make, my brothers and I still wanted land and the life that goes along with raising cattle for ourselves, and we probably wanted it even more so for our children. I'd moved to Salt Lake City to find work two decades earlier and had, for my part, lived happily in the city. I think it was the birth of my children, Belle and Joe, that first created in me a pressing need to head north, to the open country of my own childhood.

City life had offered us many things, but I always worried that my children were going without—without irrigation ditches, heavy equipment, horses, cattle, and outbuildings. I found I could drum up very little in the way of real work for Belle and Joe to do; it all seemed somewhat trivial. Yes, they picked up dog poop from the yard, they cleared the dishes from the table, and they got their own clothes into the laundry basket. But those things don't seem like real work to me. When I was their age the work that I did on the ranch—and this was not actually beyond my comprehension, even when I was little—was tied up in the very livelihood of our family and the families who were employed by us.

I wanted my children to have that same sense of purpose, and even obligation, along with a visceral connection to the earth and its plant and animal inhabitants that comes with being raised on a farm or ranch.

Matt and Brad apparently felt the same way, and when the Bar B C was sold all three of us took the money and the opportunities it gave us. Matt and his wife Carol purchased a big ranch, with buildings dating from the mid-1800s, near Laramie, and they seem to have settled fast in southeast Wyoming, four hundred miles from home. My older brother Brad, the only one of us who ended up in Jackson, purchased quite a bit of the old family ranch south of the Bar B C, and with the help of his wife, Kate, keeps it about the same as it was when we were little.

Being the middle child, I didn't know if I should go far from my origins or stay close, and I cast about for some time before I realized that Alta—despite the prejudice of my early years, and its proximity to Idaho—was perfect. It was close to the home ranch as the crow flies, yet on the other side of a great divide. It was far enough from Brad and Pete that we would have our independence and privacy, yet close enough that we could get their help with stuff and borrow their equipment. (I hate to make myself sound too calculating, but these are things I knew very well we would need.) Pete had been known to drive the four hundred miles to Laramie to help Matt put in a head gate, and I knew he'd drive four miles to help us figure out where to put a loading chute.

So when the sale of the Bar B C closed we set down the money for the Pig Farm and congratulated ourselves. Michael and I would now be able to give Belle and Joe the opportunities and advantages and chores of ranch life, just as I'd had myself, growing up in Wyoming. And Belle and Joe and I, with Michael going back and forth from Salt Lake City every weekend, have spent the years since the purchase of the Pig Farm—or at least the summers, which is when we're there full-time—trying to turn it into some semblance of a cattle ranch. The Kaufmanns have helped us and so have the Wilsons, being grateful that the new buyers wanted to keep the place in agriculture.

I only wish I could say that it's been a great success, but even with a lot of help from Lorin Wilson, it's been mostly a struggle—one that's caused me to question my abilities, reexamine my memories, and wonder, too, at my own motivations.

I

Alfalfa

For some time before we bought it, and after the pigs had gone away, the Pig Farm had been planted in canola, alfalfa, and barley, plants with which I had little familiarity. I wouldn't even have been able to identify the canola if Warren Kaufmann, the farmer to the east, hadn't told me what that bright yellow stuff was growing on a forty-acre section of our property. The only one I had any background on was alfalfa, which had negative connotations for me. Not that I knew all that much about it, but I'd learned early in my life that you didn't want cattle eating it green.

Back when we herded our cows to their summer range, past the federal government's alfalfa fields, even though they were fenced off, we had to be extra diligent about not letting our cows get their heads down under the bottom wire. Pete was always yelling at me to kick my horse, to get after the cows, to keep them moving past the fence. The cows loved the taste of it, but the rich green alfalfa produced enough stomach gas to suffocate them, Pete and Mary claimed. Throughout grade school I figured Pete's yelling at me during cattle drives was just part of a broader pattern, though, and I didn't really believe the allegations about alfalfa until I saw the evidence for myself one day.

Coming up the road one morning with the back end of the herd, which we called the drag, I saw ahead of me one of our cows lying on her side, next to the trail. I'd never known a cow to lie down like that in the middle of a cattle drive and knew something was wrong with her, but still I expected she'd arise when I rode up right next to her. Instead she lay still. I could see that her hide was stretched hard and tight over her distended stomach, and that her tongue was sticking out of her mouth, nestled in the brown dirt. The cow was already dead of bloat from the green alfalfa she'd gorged on just a mile earlier.

My horse with a sudden grasp of the situation lurched off at an angle and I was too distracted by the deadness of the cow to correct him, in fact I probably came close to falling off. I felt sorry for the poor cow, but at the same time part of me was happy; happy because there was no sign of Pete. Even if he'd still been in the vicinity, it could not have been my fault—I'd not been there to keep the cow off alfalfa—so I just grabbed onto the saddle horn and kept on going with the rest of the drag.

The truth is I had come to understand long before that day the fact that living things died, for various reasons. To the extent I was upset about it had to do partly with whether I thought it was because of something I'd done. Either way, I was somewhat used to the death of animals because Mary and Pete didn't shield us from it. The only occasion they ever did this (that I knew of) was one time in the case of an unfortunate family pet.

Pagan was one of the first dogs we had, a malamute, muscular and energetic. Pete was so fond of him that he'd carried Pagan in his saddlebag when the dog was just a puppy, and when Pagan was fully grown, Pete from time to time hitched him up to the wooden toboggan and had him pull the three of us around the ranch yard. Everyone thought he was quite the dog and well suited to ranch life. But at some point Pagan got in the habit of chasing down deer on the butte, and Pete and Mary had no way to break him of it. They wouldn't have a dog that was a menace to game and, of course, there was the chance that a fondness for killing deer might turn into a fondness for killing cattle.

One day Pagan was gone. "Where's Pagan?" we asked.

Pete was ready with an answer. "We gave him away."

"Why?"

"Because he was killing deer on the hill."

"Who'd you give him to?" we questioned. "Maybe we can visit him." We knew practically everyone in town, after all.

"No," said my father. "We gave him to a friend of mine who lives in California. A monk."

I did not want to press for further details of such an unlikely scenario. It was clear even at my young age that Mary and Pete were trying to protect our feelings by spinning a tale which so effectively removed Pagan from our world. I always imagined my father going somewhere up on the hill next to our house with his dear Pagan, on the very trails I so often walked myself, and digging a hole that I hoped I never came across evidence of, and shooting the dog in the head. He would've died painlessly, at least.

Although I didn't blame my father for shooting Pagan, I had little stomach for killing an animal myself. I learned that much in junior high school, after I shot a porcupine one winter morning. Porcupines sometimes had a habit of housing themselves in our haystacks in the wintertime, and if a cow got her muzzle in the quills she wouldn't be able to eat, and if she wasn't spotted and attended to by the vet before too long she'd starve to death. So whenever my father found a family of porcupines in a haystack, he'd shoot them and put their carcasses first in his pickup bed and then in the bone pile.

One day my brothers and I went with him to clean up a haystack that had been infested with several of the troublesome animals. My dad stirred up the porcupines, and as they came waddling out of the haystack he shot one of them. Brad shot one, I think, and then Matt, and then my dad asked me if I wanted to shoot the next one.

My heart said no, but my mouth seemed to think it should say yes, so I took the pistol from my father. I'm sure it was a small caliber, but I can still recall its cold heaviness in my hand. I took a good look at my target, the one remaining porcupine, which by then was going as fast as it could to get away from us.

But porcupines are slow. I didn't even have to take a step; all I had to do was turn 90 degrees, aim the heavy pistol, and shoot the creature in the back after it passed me, shuffling away. I think up until then I'd only shot bullets at cans on fence posts, because I was stupidly surprised at the lack of a metallic *ding* following my pull of the trigger. I feel like I heard a dull thud, but I suppose any sound of impact would in reality have been muted by the report of the gun. As I watched the stubbly animal fall softly, like a flower drooping, into the snow, I felt a swell of hate for myself but didn't say a word about it, then or at any point after that. I didn't want Brad and Matt to know I had a problem doing something we all agreed was the right thing to do, something they seemed to have no qualms about. But then I don't know what was going through their minds any more than they knew what was going through mine.

The fact that the death of animals was not unusual on a ranch never did make it feel okay—at least not for me. I realize some people might say that the purpose of a cattle ranch is, after all, dead animals, but I didn't think about it that way. Although I avoided contemplation of their fate after the cows left our ranch, I witnessed for myself that for all the time they lived on our place—which, in the case of some of the mother cows, was more than twenty years—our purpose was the opposite of dead cows. It was live cows, and healthy cows, and, I'd venture to say, even contented cows. My parents went to extremes at times to save the lives of our cows, and made a sincere effort to soothe them when they were in distress.

Whatever the seen and unseen realities of being raised on a cattle ranch might've been, after shooting the porcupine I knew I would just as soon never again, myself, be the direct cause of an animal's demise, even if it was a pest such as a porcupine, and certainly not if it was a valued cow. So decades later, when we ended up in possession of the Pig Farm, I didn't want to have any dead animals on our hands if we could avoid it.

One of the first big tasks we gave ourselves at the Pig Farm, then, was to have the ground plowed up so we could get rid of the canola, the barley, and the potentially deadly alfalfa, and plant grass for cattle pasture. I was surprised at what a difficult undertaking this was, and how, despite the fact that I'd been raised in agriculture, I understood so little about farming. I had no experience with it, actually, because there'd been no plowing or planting on the ranch where I grew up. There was simply an abundance of native grasses that for all I knew grew by themselves—with the help of our irrigator, of course, and with the help of fertilizer we didn't have to pay for, ship, or do much to spread around, given that it was manure from our own cows.

All in all we spent five years working on the Pig Farm pastures. Our neighbor Lorin Wilson, a successful third-generation farmer, had advised me right at the beginning that the best thing to do would be to replant the barley, and then the following year, to plant grass seed alongside it. This is so the barley, which would shoot up faster than the grass, would provide shade cover for the delicate new grass leaves. After two years in barley, he said, the grass would be healthy and ready to take over, and we could get out of the barley business.

I just couldn't imagine that growing plain old grass could be that difficult, though, and I wanted to get out of the barley business immediately, so I didn't heed his advice. Instead, I planted grass seed where the barley and alfalfa had been. I watered it and fertilized it and waited for it to grow, and when it didn't, I planted the fields all over again. Then the grass did grow, but slowly and with large bare spots. It wasn't until our sixth summer at the Pig Farm that the pasture grass finally came to fruition. And at that point, we were ready to ship a load of cattle from Brad's ranch to summer on our property.

He shipped just twenty-five pairs, cows and calves; even though we thought we could handle at least twice that, just so we could be sure and start off successfully. The day the cattle were delivered I took pictures of every step: the semi driving in under the M LAZY M sign; the first cow coming out of the back of the truck; and the herd funneling through the open gate into our newly fenced field. Despite my false starts I'd not only gotten the grass to finally take hold, but I'd also managed to get perimeter fences in and stock water set up. The loading chute that Pete had helped us plan worked perfectly, and Pete was there to watch the cattle come out of the truck, go through the gate, and then fan out into our beautiful green fields at a run, like a bunch of kids let into Disneyland.

I was in the cattle business.

But one day later that summer Belle and Joe and I were up at the ski resort at the base of the Tetons east of Alta, on a sunny afternoon and a good day for the kids and me to take some time off, when Brad called.

"Muffy, this is Brad." His voice on the phone that afternoon sounded as friendly as ever. "How are you doing?"

"Great, Brad." I was happy to hear from him, though surprised his call came through at all. The Grand Teton was right in between us, and

I usually had no cell-phone reception up there. "The kids and I are up at Targhee, doing some mountain-biking. What're you doing?"

"Oh, we're just at the ranch." He paused, the pleasantries done. "Umm, Muffy, Pete just called me, and I guess you have three dead cows at the Pig Farm."

"What?"

I could hardly believe what I'd just heard. Three dead cows? I'd only been gone forty-five minutes, and they were all fine when I left. How could I lose three cows in that short space of time? *Some lunatic must've shot them* was the only thing I could think of. And how in the hell did Pete know about it? And why had he called Brad instead of me? Yes, they belonged to Brad, but they were on my place and I was responsible for them.

"I'm afraid so," Brad continued. "I guess the guy who's out there working on your cattle guards spotted them and he told Pete, and Pete tried to call you but he didn't get through, so he called me."

Apparently I was the last to know. If the welder knew and my dad knew, that meant half the town of Alta probably knew before I did, including Warren Kaufmann and Lorin Wilson. That, I must admit, was part of what knotted my stomach, but the bigger part was the fact that I'd lost three cows—and all in the space of one hour. *Someone* must *have shot them,* I thought again, because I knew there hadn't been a lightning storm, and I couldn't think of anything else that would kill three cows all at once, or at least I didn't especially want to.

"I can't even believe it," I said to Brad. "I'll leave right now and get down there."

I threw the bikes in the truck and uttered a number of curse words on my way down the mountain, driving fast around the hairpin turns. When I got to the Pig Farm it didn't take long to locate the dead cows in the field, lying on their sides, all four legs sticking stiffly away from their rounded bodies. They were actually good-size calves, not cows, so only three or four months old. They were three of the biggest and healthiest calves in the whole herd. I could see that they'd not been shot, and a certain dread came over me as I began to contemplate what had most likely cut them down.

I knew that their stomachs could have swollen quickly with the accumulation of gas from decomposition, but then, it could have been caused by something else. I thought I'd gotten rid of nearly all the alfalfa, and I'd been nurturing a second planting of new grass seed for two summers. But as the grass I'd planted got higher and thicker that summer, I'd noticed as I walked the fields a few too many round alfalfa leaves volunteering up between the blades, and ultimately overtaking the grass in some spots. Even though I'd then gone straight to Driggs and bought a truckload of Bloat Guard, there was no way to ensure that every animal ate as much of it as they needed to provide an antidote for the gas-producing protein of alfalfa.

I still didn't want to believe it was alfalfa, though. So I had the vet come over from Victor, Idaho, to do a full necropsy on one of the calves that evening.

I'd had enough dealings with Dr. Summer Winger to know that she was knowledgeable about cows and that she didn't jump to conclusions, and I appreciated her showing up after work hours with her vet kit. She was a small woman, blonde and pretty and about my height, but I outweighed her by at least ten pounds, and she asked for my help to hold the dead calf's legs apart as she inserted her Buck knife and cut the length of its belly.

One by one Summer examined every organ, pointing out to me what was what and how things worked, and eliminating various possible causes of death as she went along. When she opened the stomach sac we could see about a twenty-pound bolus of bright green feed, and her remark confirmed for me the conclusion we were probably headed for.

"Boy," she said, "that's some rich stuff."

Ultimately it was the esophagus that provided the definitive sign. Summer split it lengthwise with her scalpel and we looked at the inside of it. She showed me how below a certain point it was a healthy pink, but there was clearly a line above which the tissue was white. White, due to lack of oxygen. Lack of oxygen, due to bloat. Bloat, due to green alfalfa, which was obviously still as deadly as I'd always known it to be.

Later that night I undertook the bitter task of recording in my Pig Farm journal how I'd lost the three big calves. Pete had suggested to me when we bought the place that I write events down, so that I'd always be able to compare one year to another and know what worked and what didn't. Granddad had made this same suggestion to Pete when Pete had married my mother and come to the ranch, and he'd found it was valuable advice.

After putting the day's regrettable occurrences in writing, I stood by myself in the kitchen and cried with my head in my hands and my elbows on the countertop. I felt much more disgusted with myself than when I'd shot the porcupine. The three calves had been in my care. I thought about the mother of one of the calves, and the way she had watched us, cutting up the carcass of her offspring. She'd stood by defensively, sniffing the air as we put all the organs topsy-turvy back inside, and she'd stood there bellowing as Summer had sewn the animal back together crudely but effectively with bailing twine. She'd been a devoted mother, and her calf had been so healthy and so strong, just that morning.

I was crying that night in sadness over the three lost calves, but I was probably crying more in frustration at my own incompetence, my overreach, my inability to farm something as simple as grass. And I was asking myself why I'd created the whole situation, starting with buying the property; no one else had asked me to sign up for any of it.

Why had I bought the Pig Farm in the first place and saddled myself with all that work, which, apparently, I had no business doing? I'd told everyone including myself that Michael and I had done it mostly for Belle and Joe—all the real work it would give them, and that high-minded bit about a visceral connection to the earth and its plant and animal inhabitants—but six years into it I wasn't too sure how much they cared. They weren't crying in the kitchen. And I didn't even know any more if my children's welfare had been my true motivation in the first place. Either way, I was ready to sell the whole 125 acres to the highest bidder. It had me in over my head. If I'd been so hell-bent on having a place in Wyoming, I asked myself, why couldn't I have bought something manageable? Like, I don't know—a cabin?

The answers didn't come to me that night, and the next morning the dead calves were hauled to the dump. And although I doubled my outlay on Bloat Guard, a few weeks later one of the sweet mother cows also keeled over and died of bloat, and Brad and I decided at that point to cut our losses. We rounded up the cows and calves, and Brad brought his cattle truck back over the Tetons to load them up and take them home.

Shortly after that, the summer was over. Our whole family left the Pig Farm to head back to Salt Lake City for the school year, to lives filled not with big skies and rolling pastures but with streets and buildings and traffic. Lives populated not with cattle and horses but with more than a million other people. An environment which at that point I actually felt more at ease in, because I didn't have so much to worry about. Not irrigating, not fencing, not cattle guards, and not calves with their legs sticking up in the air. And I wondered whether the Pig Farm, once it was closed up for the winter, might in fact be salable—if there might be a farmer who'd want to put the whole thing back in canola, barley, and alfalfa.

But near the end of October I received a package in the mail that gave me at least part of the answer as to why I'd done what I'd done . . . why I'd been so sure I had to have a cattle ranch. And why, perhaps, I'd been flailing.

The package came from my friend Kathy. I'd grown up with her in Jackson, and since we'd been introduced before either one of us was out of diapers, we were kind of thrust together as friends. We hadn't been able to shake each other ever since and hadn't wanted to. She was someone who'd been not only a friend to me, but also a helper in both business and personal matters to Pete and Leslie and to Brad and Kate, so she was acquainted with our family from several angles.

I could see by the return address that the package was coming from Kathy before I opened it, but had no idea what she might have sent to me. It wasn't close to my birthday or any other gift-giving occasion. When I got through the tape and into the cardboard box I could see that it wasn't a gift, in any case; it was just some things stuffed into a kitchen garbage bag. There was a note on top of the bag which read: "Muffy, I've had these things for some time and thought they should go to you."

So I pulled open the plastic bag and what I saw there was clothing— a pair of jeans first of all, but they were cut all along the length of the leg—and it struck me. It struck me that here was my mother's last outfit of clothes. Questions about how Kathy came by them, and why she chose that particular moment in time to send them to me after all those years, were shunted aside by the fact that I held them in my hands.

Mary's jeans, still matted with dirt from the pasture where she'd fallen under the weight of her horse fourteen years before, were cut jaggedly from the hem through to the waist on both legs. Her ivory blouse, her fleece top, and even her underwear were there, all cut haphazardly through from top to bottom. Only her socks were still whole. My mouth opened involuntarily, and into my mind came a jumpy silent film of those moments when some anonymous medical person must have been trying in vain to save my mother's life, racing in an ambulance from the cattle grounds to the hospital in town. Or was she already gone by then? Were the clothes cut off at the hospital, when it was already too late? As I held Mary's soft ruined blouse in my hands I didn't think so, because the cuts themselves said *hurry, hurry*.

Both the shock and then the plunging grief of my mother's sudden departure were still there waiting for me if I wanted to get them out of their compartment, apparently, and so was the self-pity at having lost her without warning.

And what was also there, looming so large that I felt it might crowd me right out of the basement laundry room in which I stood, was the fact that much of my grief and self-pity had to do not with her death, but with the fact that I was still trying to measure up to her level. Here in my hands was the last outfit of a woman whose boots I would surely never fill. Her life had been that of a rugged Wyoming cattle rancher, who came from a long line of rugged Wyoming cattle ranchers, chronicled in newspaper articles, magazine pieces, and a few television programs. Even her death had been pure heroism in most people's eyes: a tragic fall from horseback in the early morning, on her birthday, of all days, as she moved a big herd of cattle to their summer range with the majestic Tetons rising in rock and snow behind her.

No wonder I'd been insisting that a pig farm could be turned into a cattle ranch. In the vainest way imaginable I was trying to live up to my birthright.

That I wasn't succeeding seemed painfully clear to me as I stood there in the laundry room with the cardboard box and the cut-up clothing, recollecting the loss of three calves the previous summer. But also clear to me, more than at any other time in my life, was that I had a birthright I missed acutely and loved deeply. I loved it to my bones, even if only looking back on it.

And even if looking back on it was starting to look like the best chance I had of doing it justice.

2

The Lower Ranch, Pete and Mary

A LOT OF THINGS SEEMED REALLY HUGE TO ME WHEN I WAS LITTLE, AND then when I grew up I discovered they'd shrunk, sometimes to as little as half their previous size. I noted this when I drove by my old grade school in Jackson after I'd graduated from college. It was the most imposing building of my early years, and the first large building I'd ever spent any time in. But this edifice which I'd thought housed endless corridors and classrooms turned out to be drab and narrow, and so low to the ground that it struggled to leave the pavement.

That yank to my perspective didn't happen with the ranch I grew up on, though, because in that case, it was nearly as large as it seemed. Its dimensions were more dizzying when I was little than those of the grade school. In fact, to me, its size was its chief attribute; I could hardly hope to walk across it. The part we lived on was about 2,000 acres, and the two ranches held by our family to the north of it were each that same size, and the views from most places on the property made it seem even bigger. On some days in the middle of December you could look north across the fields through clear air that had been zapped nearly empty of all its particulates—at temperatures of 30 or 40 below zero—and see sharply the peaks of mountain ranges more than fifty miles away. Land, land, and more land was what I saw—what I sometimes felt I was drowning in.

Six thousand acres is not that big a ranch if, for instance, you're on the high flats outside of Laramie, Wyoming. Ranches in other parts of Wyoming—and of course Texas and Montana, not to mention Australia—can go up into the hundreds of thousands of acres. But in that valley southeast of the Tetons our ranch was big, even to adults, and it was endless to me.

Initially cobbled together by my great-grandfather on Mary's side, my family's ranches in Jackson Hole, with the Grand Tetons as a backdrop, were literally the stuff of postcards and paintings. The landscape wasn't just beautiful, however; with its natural attributes, it was a good place to raise cattle. It was bordered east and west by long, semi-forested buttes. The rumbling Gros Ventre River ran crosswise over it and the willow-lined spring creeks—creeks that came up from the earth and didn't freeze over in winter—ran the length of it.

And it had, over the course of a hundred years, increased both in size and in productivity thanks to the hardscrabble efforts of my great-grandparents, my grandparents, several great-aunts and -uncles, my own parents, and dozens of ranch hands, some legendary and others long forgotten. They toiled to dig irrigation ditches, build fences, clear pastures, erect barns and corrals, and turn the part of it that had been sagebrush flats into a cowboy's—and, I would think, a cow's—dream come true, which is what the ranch was by the time I came along.

Across the curve of the dirt road to the east of the house we lived in was a long, irregular mountain named East Gros Ventre Butte, after the Gros Ventre River, after the Gros Ventre Indians—or at least, the Native Americans who were referred to that way by French trappers and eventually everyone else without any nod to the fact that they called themselves *A'aninin* in their own language. The Gros Ventre Indians were long departed by the time I came along, but early on I was informed by someone that the phrase *gros ventre* meant "big belly" in French, so I always had what I thought was a clear picture of them in my mind. And without necessarily saying anything to Brad or Matt, I kept an eye out for them when my brothers and I camped overnight in the hills to the east of our house.

East Gros Ventre Butte is a glacial moraine populated mainly with grass and sagebrush, but also with thick stands of aspens in the gullies and evergreens on the north-facing slopes. We had a barbed-wire fence stretched up the western side of this long mountain, a fence which did a 90-degree turn and ran along our property line at the top, ticked south for a few miles and then coursed back down to the valley in an effort to contain the twenty or thirty Hereford bulls we pastured on the hill.

The world was big for the bulls, too. East Gros Ventre Butte provided them with a realm that was steep but large, maybe ten times more country than what they really needed, and I wonder, looking back now, if that excess of ground made them feel self-important, because that's how they came across. I could lie in my bed at night during the spring before they'd been trucked up to the summer range to mix with the cows, and hear them test their voices, bellering at one another across the draw. Sometimes, even though they were on the other side of the horse pasture and across the road from my bedroom window, perhaps 150 yards away, I could hear their footsteps rattling the round rocks of the creek bank as they came for water in the dark, arguing.

More than once these miscreants broke through the barbed-wire fence at the very top corner of their hill pasture, where they enjoyed congregating at the highest point they could reach on the butte, and then they would lumber in currents of dust down the other side of the hill into the town of Jackson. The bulls liked it up at the top, for some reason. Perhaps it was the fifty-mile view. Or perhaps they preferred to be at the point where they were farthest removed from society. Whatever their reasons, the ground in that corner where the north-south and the east-west fences came together on the top of East Gros Ventre Butte was always scoured bare of grass and sagebrush by their split hooves and bulky hindquarters. They spent so much time in that high place, milling around and rubbing up against each other, that a breach in the fence from time to time was inevitable.

When they did bully themselves through the barbed wire and go down into town, it was the friendly employees of the A&W drive-through restaurant, then located at the north end of Jackson, who usually gave us a call. Since the east side of the mountain was too steep for herding the bulls back up to the fence break, my parents had to load their horses into a pickup truck with a stock rack and drive it, along with a cattle truck that would accommodate the bulls, around the south end of the butte into town.

Then they'd round up the animals on horseback and herd them slowly, which is to say at whatever pace the bulls chose, down the street, past the shops and restaurants, past the Cowboy Bar, past the Antler Motel, all the way to the rodeo grounds on the south end of town. The rodeo grounds were the only place in the town of Jackson with corrals and a loading chute, so they were the practical terminating point of these lawless outings and it was better than trying to herd the bulls all the way home. They didn't herd that well.

At the western margin of our ranch was another glacial leaving, West Gros Ventre Butte, loping along from north to south opposite its brother. West Gros Ventre Butte was where our horses wintered, finding natural protection from the wind and snow in thick clumps of aspen trees. The aspens congregated closely in the gullies, the hillside furrows into which the melted snow drained and soaked just enough to give the tree roots the moisture they needed to grow, and they provided shelter for our horses in winter.

Except for the few that were very young, or had problems which needed to be addressed by the vet, or were kept near the house for the intermittent bit of winter wrangling, we didn't see much of our horses during the winter. They foraged for themselves on the hillsides, and ate hay left over from what was put out on a daily basis for the calves. Then we rounded them up in the spring and brought them back to the corrals at the ranch buildings and took stock of how well they'd wintered. The phrase "He looks like he wintered well" was my grandfather's tongue-in-cheek way of referring to a person who was overweight, and it gave me the impression that it was beneficial for animals and humans to have lean times. Every once in a while one of the oldest horses wouldn't come back, and that seemed like not only a natural occurrence, but a relatively good way to go.

In our family, horses that got to be too old to ride weren't typically sold anyway. They were pastured on the ranch, keeping the company they'd always known, until they died of natural causes.

In between the two long formations I've just described, East and West Gros Ventre Buttes, lay the hayfields of our ranch, wide ground that had been conveniently graded flat by an ancient advancing river of ice and gravel, 2,000 feet thick in its heyday, about 200,000 years before my great-grandfather got there. These level hayfields seemed to reach out forever, north and south, when I was little, broken up by just a few features, widely scattered: the willowed banks of a spring creek, traversing the ranch east to west about half a mile north of our house; irrigation canals and distributary ditches, which were hardly visible when the hay was high; and the two-story white house where the hired man, Roy Martin, lived with his family, a mile to the north. And, although their numbers dwindled over the course of our long winter, until spring you could see round-top haystacks built not with bales but with loose, mounded hay held together just by its own weight; the slat fence around the bottom served mainly to keep animals out of them.

But all of these features seemed very far away. The hayfields stretched before me, and the mountains away to the north were so far as to be a drab and imprecise blue in color. It was the sky, I felt, that stretched right down to me. It was the sky that often seemed close at hand, not far and compartmentalized the way it is where I live now, in the city. I often walked to the top of East Gros Ventre Butte by myself in the summer just to see the long view, and also because I wanted at times to be completely alone, and the top of the butte was a place where your solitude was guaranteed if you stayed out of the way of the bulls. Not even our dog wanted to walk up that far with me. Once I was atop the butte a trick of perspective made me feel that I was approximately as high as the top of the Grand Teton, ten miles to the northwest and 7,000 feet above me.

Mary had a copper cowbell she'd ring if she wanted me to come off the hill, or my brothers to come in from the shop for some reason, such as lunch. The cowbell was only about four inches high, including the handle, but when she started wagging it you could hear it literally a mile away. The air was clear, and most of the time there wasn't anyone or anything else between us and town, five miles away, making noise. So the cowbell called me home from however far away I was, and there was almost never a time when I didn't heed its call.

Home was the two-story log house that my great-grandmother and great-grandfather had moved into in the 1940s, after my great-grandfather had purchased that part of the ranch from Major C. C. Moseley.

Major Moseley had purchased it from the Charters, who had purchased it from a Mr. Bill Redmond, and it was Redmond who had settled the land in 1894. Jackson Hole had a relatively inhospitable climate and extremely rugged surroundings, so it was settled later than a lot of other frontier towns, and 1894 was early by Jackson Hole standards—three years before even my own great-grandfather arrived in the valley.

We referred to the portion of the ranch I grew up on sometimes as the Lower Ranch and just as often as the Charter Place. Bert Charter was a well-known character whose reputation was enhanced—if you liked that sort of thing (which I did)—by what many believed was a shady past. He'd been our family's neighbor long before my time, since in 1916 my great-grandparents had purchased the north end of Mr. Redmond's property at the same time Mr. Charter had purchased the south end, although in time—1947 to be exact—we bought that land as well, finally reuniting the Redmond property into one ranch again.

It was complicated, but a ranch the size of my ancestors' could rarely be put together in one transaction. This is partly because Jackson Hole had been divided among many homesteaders near the turn of the century, and partly because it would've been hard to come up with that much money at one time. Unlike my great-grandfather, however, Mr. Charter paid cash when he bought his ranch from Mr. Redmond, which to some was evidence of Mr. Charter's involvement with outlaws—namely Butch Cassidy (or at least that was the rumor).

One man who had a firsthand account that adds to the legend of Bert Charter was a gentleman named Bob Crisp. Bob was a figure who looked like he'd come out of a Frederic Remington painting, bowlegged and ruddy from the eyebrows down. He was an accomplished bronc rider, and when I knew him he was an employee of a ranching neighbor and also a range rider for the Bacon Creek Association, of which our family was a part. The Bacon Creek Association was formed by a group of ranchers to lease grazing land forty miles east of Jackson from the federal government, and a cowboy such as Bob Crisp was needed to ride herd behind those thousands of cattle during the four months they spent every summer on the enormous fenceless range.

My brother Brad, though just one year older than me, knew Bob quite a bit better than I ever did because he spent more time herding cows with him. I was typically riding with the drag, just as I was the day I came upon the bloated cow, whereas Brad was a bit more likely to be miles ahead with the front of the herd, riding with cowboys the ilk of Bob Crisp. Though Bob was probably in an ilk by himself.

Bob had worked for Bert Charter when Bob was a young man. One of the duties Mr. Charter sometimes asked him to perform was to wrangle ten or fifteen horses in the evening and leave them in the corral with the gate closed. Sometimes, according to Bob, when he'd go out in the mornings, there would be the same number of horses, but some of them would be different horses, with the outlines of a saddle blanket and cinch still marked in sweat on their hides.

It was appealing when I heard that story (and still is) to picture a band of on-the-run outlaws coming through in the night and swapping their worn-out horses for fresh ones, right on our own ranch.

When I was little I didn't understand why we continued to refer to our location as the Charter Place, and actually wondered if Mr. Charter might still have some proprietary interest in it. If I should be extra careful, say, when using tools in the shop that might still belong to Bert Charter. Now I realize (and the Pig Farm is a good example of the fact) that place names can stick rather arbitrarily, and many of them did. The Charter Place wasn't the only name that didn't make sense to me.

It was easy to feel lost when you didn't know what (or where) people were referring to. There was one piece of ground that had been for quite a while the bull pasture, and everybody called it that long after we started pasturing the bulls elsewhere. We had another large piece of land north of where we lived which we referred to as the "school section," because it had been owned by the State of Wyoming at one point for the benefit of their school trust fund. But I didn't know that then, and I didn't know how most other things got to be called what they were. The school section was one of the many place names that indicated something completely different than what it actually was, thereby mystifying me.

I wasn't going to ask anyone for an explanation, though, and I didn't ask anyone to explain why we called the place where we lived, in addition to the Charter Place, the "Lower Ranch," which was another designation that for years made no sense to me. I was nearly out of elementary school by the time that deficiency was remedied by my mother.

"I'm going to ride my bike down to Martins'," I told Mary one Saturday afternoon.

The Martins, who worked for us, lived a mile north on what we called the Double T, part of our ranch but its own place, too, an enclave of buildings including a couple of small houses, some sheds, and two barns, along with a system of corrals that worked particularly well for branding and vaccinating. We'd purchased the property we called the Double T from Mr. Redmond at the same time Bert Charter had purchased the land just south of us that bore his name. But the Double T brand itself hadn't been Mr. Redmond's. As I've said, brands don't always stay with places, and my family had acquired the Double T brand along with some cattle from a man named Mr. Miller, when my great-grandparents purchased his property on what is now the National Elk Refuge (a picturesque and often photographed piece of property—though my great-grandmother in her memoirs referred to it as "our swamp ranch"). I still don't know why the Double T name was eventually given to the particular piece of property a mile north of our house or why it stuck. But I never called it the Double T anyway. I called it the Martins'.

"You don't mean *down* to Martins'," Mary replied. "You mean up."

"What?"

My mother was a ranch wife—not a housewife, but a ranch wife. Having grown up there, having helped run the place from the time she was small, she was married to the ranch as much as to her husband. She was strong enough to throw a fifty-pound bale of hay into the back of a pickup in spite of her diminutive frame; she was comfortable riding horseback all day and looked good in a cowboy hat; she could operate all kinds of heavy machinery, and was no stranger to man's work. She also made sixteen loaves of bread at a time.

She turned from the spot in front of the kitchen counter where she was engaged in a scuffle with some flour, water, and yeast. She looked at me with wide eyes to convey her amazement and probably dismay that I didn't seem to know the difference between two concepts as fundamental as *up* and *down*.

"Which way," she asked in a plain voice, "does the water flow?"

I had to picture myself wading the creek for a moment but I did know the answer to that: Water flowed from the north to the south in Spring Gulch, the valley where our ranches lay, and where we lived was close to the south end. The Martins, as I said, were a mile north. Suddenly there in the kitchen I grasped the fact that their place must be a bit higher, and that the Bar B C, our ranch another four miles to the north, must be even higher than that. So where we lived was, in fact, lower. And that explained why the ranch north of the Bar B C was sometimes referred to as the Upper Ranch. So if I rode my bike to Martins' I was going upstream; I was actually, though imperceptibly, gaining altitude. I thought that was so logical and interesting! I also thought it was too bad I'd lived a whole decade on a place called the Lower Ranch and never asked what that meant.

I didn't let my mom know any of that, though; I just said "Oh," and left for the Martins'.

I thought concealing my amazement at this and other revelations—along with not asking Mary or Pete most of the questions that occurred to me—was a good way to avoid looking dumb. So I looked dumb a good portion of the time, and learned most things while growing up by having my course corrected after first going wrong, most often in front of someone.

How my brother Brad usually seemed to know what to do in so many situations eluded me. Though he was only a year older than I was, I looked up to him as though he was our parents' age. And I was slightly less averse to asking him questions than I was to asking the actual adults, so I did learn quite a bit from him. He taught me how to read before I went to kindergarten. My parents' friends were surprised that I could read at the age of four, but they were incredulous when told that Brad, at the age of five, was the one who'd taught me. (I don't think my parents cared whether we learned to read at age four, five, six, or whatever.)

More important to me over the years was that Brad taught me survival skills: how to find ditch crossings, how to hammer nails, how to leverage your body weight to stretch a wire gate closed—and often the names of things, whether they made sense to me or not. So I don't mean survival in terms of staying alive; I mean survival in terms of not continually looking like a greenhorn, a dude, or, as we sometimes referred to them, a drugstore cowboy, meaning someone who puts on his hat, boots, and big belt buckle and loiters in front of Jackson Drug on the busiest corner in town, hoping to be mistaken for the real thing.

I so feared and loathed the label of drugstore cowboy that I never even wore my cowboy hat and boots to town unless I was with a group of real cowboys, and the only times that seemed to happen were the infrequent occasions when my parents took the whole cattle-driving crew out to the Wagon Wheel Restaurant for breakfast after we'd finished a cattle drive or branding. I don't know that I looked very authentic compared to most of them; for one thing, I didn't chew tobacco. But no one looked as wonderfully authentic as my father Pete.

Pete was born and raised by a skiing family in Vermont, and he was a noted alpine ski racer but was overshadowed by his sister, Andrea Mead Lawrence, given the fact that she had won two gold medals in the 1952 Winter Olympics in Oslo. After leaving the East Coast he followed a friend from the US Ski Team west to Wyoming, and eventually to Jackson, where he became a cowboy. Unlike most newcomers he became a real cowboy, one who would never have been mistaken for a drugstore cowboy even if he had loitered on the corner.

When I say *cowboy*, I mean he was an expert with cattle and horses, that being the fundamental measuring stick, but he was also a cowboy in the John Wayne sense, the movie-star sense. For several years of my childhood he rode a light palomino called Stinger, a well-muscled and aggressive horse, one I wouldn't have dreamed of trying to ride, or even put a halter on. Stinger was one of those horses who could move sideways fast, which my own horses thankfully were not in the habit of doing, unless, for instance, they unexpectedly came upon a dead cow on the trail.

Stinger always looked handsome and dressy, if a bit intimidating, and I can say the same about my father. Pete wore a silk bandanna tied around his neck every day, either a black or a white one, as most of the cowboys did. Not as an expression of style, but because having your neck covered made almost more of a difference as to whether or not you were cold than a jacket did. Pete wore only collared, ironed shirts with pearl snaps, and though most of them were heavy blue denim, he had a variety of fancier colors, too. You didn't see him in T-shirts or even short sleeves.

When I was a toddler some people from an advertising agency in New York City arrived in Jackson Hole looking for a cowboy to help them sell Camel cigarettes for their client, R.J. Reynolds. The sheriff told them they ought to be introduced to Pete Mead, and he gave them directions to the ranch on Spring Gulch Road. The advertising men ended up at my grandparents' house, which was the first building you arrived at coming from town, but after greeting them, Granddad said that Pete wasn't there.

"He's just up the road working cattle right now," Granddad said, "but he'll be coming in for lunch pretty soon if you want to wait."

They did, and fifteen minutes later my father rode snappily into the yard on Stinger, his silk neckerchief, I can imagine, just catching the breeze. He hopped off the regal palomino, strode over to the strangers, and as they stared, pulled a pack of unfiltered Camels out of his shirt pocket and lit one up. From what Granddad said the men from J. Walter Thompson were nearly brought to their knees, and naturally they took the whole incident as a sign. For the next few years Pete was featured in Camel's print and television campaigns as "Pete Mead, Ranch Manager," though RJR never completely capitalized on the possibilities of a Western cigarette brand; that was left to Marlboro.

The advertising men that day were not looking for an actor, they were looking for the real thing. And they knew when they met Pete that he was it, but they couldn't have known to what extent. A story about a time he had to retrieve some stranded cows from the range on Bacon Creek would have illustrated it for them.

For most of my childhood I thought it was a pretty large contribution on my part that I helped to gather and herd the cattle all the way home from the Bacon Creek Range, forty miles above the ranch, but it was a long time before I understood the actual consequences when we left an animal behind. And what struck me about the following account when I heard about it years later—in addition to the adventure and courage it depicted—was the fact that I'd not known anything about the event at the time it happened.

It was a year in the mid-1960s, just before Christmas, and Pete was accompanied by Brownie Brown, patriarch of a family who shared the range with us. Brownie was a generation older than Pete and had taken to him like a father as much as a business partner and neighbor, and Pete, whose own father had died young, looked up to him.

Pete and Brownie rode up alongside the Gros Ventre River with their hat brims down against the blizzard all day long, not stopping for lunch, wanting to make the Dew Place by dark. (The Dew Place was a log encampment used as a stopover for our summer herders, and it would provide shelter for the two men and their horses.)

They had two horses each: one to ride to the Dew Place, and their best cow horse on a lead behind, which they'd use to locate and gather the lost cows. The snow, once they got to the Bar Double R, twenty miles from home, was up to their horses' chests, so it was slow, hard, and cold going, and it was dark by the time they covered the next twenty miles to the Dew. They spent the night in the old Dew cabin and were able to shelter and rest their horses in one of the decrepit log sheds to the west of it.

When they got up the next morning they had some idea where to look for the yearlings based on the report of a pilot who'd spotted them from the air a few days before. The cows were not only above Bacon Creek—they were also above Heifer Creek, further to the northeast, and once the stream had frozen they wouldn't cross it. So they were stuck, and there was no way they'd be able to dig up enough feed to make it through the winter. Pete and Brownie, riding their top cow horses, found them without too much trouble about midday, sheltered up in the trees. They rode up on them and gathered them up pretty easily, but even with the cowboys pushing them, the cows wouldn't cross the ice. They were smart not to want to go out on the ice, but it just so happened that in this case it was a safe crossing.

Pete said they drove them as hard as they could before resigning themselves to the fact that they'd have to rope them and drag them, one at a time, across the frozen stream. They weren't going to abandon the poor animals for the winter—not only because it would have been cruel, but because a cow at that time was worth two or three hundred dollars, and it was money neither the Brown family nor ours could afford to ride away from.

By the time they got all the yearlings dragged across the ice of Heifer Creek it was late in the day. Pete said that with almost no visibility in the blowing snow, they started to wonder if they were still even headed back for the Dew Place, and it was so cold he didn't know if they'd make it there alive. They knew there was an old hunting cabin to the northeast of them, so they got behind the cows and rode for that. They made it to the hunting cabin only to discover that the door was padlocked, but they were desperate. Pete got his pistol out of his holster and shot the lock, and he and Brownie holed up in the cabin until they were thawed out enough, and the weather cleared enough, that they could make the ride back to the Dew Place with the cows, who had no incentive at any point in time to run off. It wasn't like they'd turned wild; they just hadn't trusted the ice of Heifer Creek.

Eventually the cattle were driven all the way home through forty miles of Wyoming winter, but it was rough going and it hadn't warmed up any. Pete had brought a cut-up steak to eat on the way down the trail, but when he stopped at Crystal Creek, the halfway point, to change horses and eat a bite, he discovered as he dug the meat out of his pocket that the pieces were as solid as wood; frozen. At one point Pete's horse fell in a pit of snow and threw my father over his front end, and then the horse, desperate to free himself, stuffed Pete deep into the cold snow as he scrambled over the top of him.

This is what the advertising men from J. Walter Thompson could not have known when they hired Pete to be the Camel man based on that fabulous first impression. My father, though he'd married into the ranching operation, felt responsible for every animal that was a part of it, to the point of risking his well-being, if not his life.

Though I suppose if he hadn't felt that way he wouldn't have gotten along with my mother very well, because for Mary the ranch was the world.

Pete and Mary did get along, especially considering how much time they spent with each other. They did almost everything together from herding cattle to putting up hay. The ranch was not a sexist environment, mostly because that would've been impractical, so they shared the responsibilities of being boss. It's true that my mother wasn't usually the one with the welding torch and my father was never seen rolling out pie dough, but their authority was equal, and they both put in the same physical and mental effort.

I didn't always get along with Mary myself, for several reasons, but the most fundamental one, I think, had to do with my feelings of inadequacy. I'm not sure if that means I resented feeling inadequate and took it out on her, or if I was, in fact, inadequate and could tell I disappointed her, or if I actually was adequate but didn't have enough people telling me so. I know I did care about our cows. Actually, I had a nearly debilitating soft spot for all animals. I cared about the ranch, too. But I didn't feel the kind of ownership that Pete displayed by riding two straight days after four head of cattle in the snow, and I'm sure it showed. I simply didn't think many things were under my control, so I was more apt to be passive—to stand by and observe the fact that things were going wrong, or were going right without necessarily doing anything to have an effect on it.

In fact, though one part of me bought into the idea that I had a legitimate claim to the wide-ranging domain of the Lower Ranch, another part of me felt like an interloper. I had the run of the place and took some advantage of that while at the same time worrying that I might overstep my bounds. One fall afternoon, when I was just barely old enough to be left home alone, I told Mary when she came back that a man had come knocking on the door while she was gone, to find out if he could go hunting for elk on our ranch.

"Well," she asked, "did you tell him yes or no?"

It wasn't the first time she'd indicated that she expected me to have an opinion on that sort of thing, but I hadn't had one. I'd told the man he had to come back later when my parents were home. I'm pretty sure Mary was disappointed by the way I'd passed the buck, and subsequent to this incident, you'd think I would have inquired as to whether it was or was not okay for people to hunt on the ranch, and if so, what the restrictions might be. But I didn't do that. Instead I just hoped I wouldn't be home alone the next time a hunter came knocking on the door.

It's true that I was only a child, but I know how Grammy described my mother's approach, when Mary was a child.

My grandmother told me, several years after Mary's death, that during World War II many of the ranch hands were called into service. One summer they didn't have enough hands to get the hay in, so Mary and her younger brother Peter had been helping, even though they were only grade-school age. When it came time for them to go back to school in September, Mary said she wasn't going, because the haying wasn't done. After a family discussion it was decided that my grandmother would let her household chores go by the wayside during the school day, and she would drive the tractor Mary had been using to rake the hay, an arrangement to which Mary only reluctantly agreed.

Grammy described to me how she would be bouncing along in the tractor seat in her straw hat, getting the hay raked into rows so it could be dried, picked up, and stacked, and she would see the school bus coming up Spring Gulch Road in the afternoon. "The bus wouldn't even come to a full stop," Grammy told me, "before Mary would jump out and run with her school books into the field. She couldn't wait to get up in the seat and behind the wheel to take over."

We had one portrait of Mary that had been taken in grade school, with her bright eyes and blond hair, so as Grammy spoke I pictured Mary in that particular dress and laced shoes doing as Grammy described, running with a load of books across the hay ground, nice clothes being the last thing to keep her off the tractor.

By the time I heard that story from my grandmother I hadn't lived on the ranch for years, and my mother had been dead for several years, but my grandmother's description of Mary as a grade-schooler begged a comparison with myself as a youngster. I didn't remember going to do my work at a run when I was a fifth-grader. In fact, I don't think I had a tractor-driving job at the age of ten the way Mary had; I don't think Pete had me driving a tractor until I was twelve or thirteen.

I asked myself why I would have been less able, less of a contributor, than my mother had been. Was it because my parents, who I thought were quite demanding of me, were actually going easy? Was it because when I was driving a tractor our country was not at war, so I didn't have that as a backdrop to increase the importance of my contribution? Or were Mary and I just made differently from the get-go?

I don't know, I guess, how differently we were made. But I suspect it might have had as much to do with *when* we were made as *how*, the difference between being born in 1935 and being born in 1960. The origins of the ranch—the struggle to put it together—all of that was a generation closer to my mother than it was to me. It had been during her lifetime that a good chunk of the property had been acquired. And she understood, perhaps, that something which had taken so much sacrifice and toil to put together could also come apart for lack of it.

As for me, I never saw any part of the ranch coming together; by the time I came along it was just there, and had been, so I imagined, since time immemorial. I did not imagine that it could ever come apart. For any reason. And besides, I usually thought I was working plenty hard. It would be years before I came to appreciate how most of the really hard work—the work of building the ranch up in the first place—had been done before my time. Not just by my parents, but also by my grandparents, and perhaps even more so by my great-grandparents, P.C. and Sylvia.

3

Sylvia and P.C., Cliff and Martha

I THOUGHT OF THE CHARTERS' HOUSE, THE ONE WE LIVED IN, AS QUITE large. I always remembered it that way even though I now know it was as modest as most 1920s houses, especially those in rural locations. It was constructed of logs and had three bedrooms upstairs and one on the main floor. Most people thought it was wonderful, the quintessential Jackson Hole dwelling, but my mother had mixed feelings about that.

"Don't have a log house," Mary said to me one time. This was nearly as irrelevant as her telling me, when I was little, not to have chickens, because at the time she told me not to have a log house, I was in no position to have a house of any kind. I was probably in junior high, and I think I was helping her vacuum the carpeting in the living room.

But this was different than the edict about chickens, because although we didn't have chickens when I was growing up, we did in fact live in a log house. So I found it somewhat alarming that she would advise me not to have one, and I didn't just accept it the same way I'd accepted the pronouncement about chickens. I asked for an explanation.

"Flies," she said.

And she went on to describe how the old logs, with their hand-hewn chinking and loosely stuffed insulation, were full of flies all winter long— flies you couldn't get to with the pointy end of a vacuum hose. Mary could look the other way when it came to cow manure, afterbirth, sour milk, and dead animals, but she did not like flies.

Notwithstanding my mother's misgivings about flies, the Charters' house—which after their departure became my great-grandparents' house, and eventually our house—had been a landmark structure at one time, at least by the standards of sparsely populated Spring Gulch Road. When my great-grandparents, P.C. and Sylvia, had moved into the house in the 1940s, it meant quite a bit to my great-grandmother.

By that time Sylvia had spent many years of her life in bunkhouses and tiny cabins, and, during the summers, in tents or wagons. She'd worked her way through quite a few spring seasons, serving meals out of a covered wagon to all the ranch hands and family members who were following the cows to their summer range. She'd had six children without the benefit of hospitalization, each of whom, against the odds of that era, survived. And when she finally had the opportunity to live in a proper house she'd enjoyed having it proper.

The family bedrooms were upstairs, the guest room was on the main floor, and downstairs was a tiny, dark cellar in place of a real basement, barely big enough to accommodate its hodgepodge contents including quite a few pairs of skis, and the electric pump which delivered water from the creek just east of the house.

One of the more deluxe features of Sylvia's house was a formal dining room. The dining and living rooms had been paneled in thick planks of knotty pine right over the logs, and given a coat of varnish that, by the time I lived there, had aged to the color of apple cider. Behind the paneling there were mice as well as flies, but it had the same old glow as the handmade trestle table and benches, also of pine, and the massive buffet, all of which my mother eventually inherited along with the house. I'm not saying that I myself thought there was anything deluxe about our dining room, or the rest of our house, for that matter. For my great-grandmother, however, the dining room was a long-overdue luxury.

(I reminisced about our respective grandparents and great-grandparents one time with a friend whose ancestors had homesteaded in Cody, Wyoming, and whose family stories had many parallels with mine. My friend Charlie could appreciate the emphasis my great-grandmother Sylvia had put on a dining room and told me his own grandmother wouldn't even go on a picnic. She'd worked too hard for too many years, said Charlie, to be able to afford a dining room with a table to put the food on and eat from, and after that she'd refused to eat on the ground.)

I knew my own great-grandmother well; she lived until I was fifteen, to the age of ninety, and I loved her company. But she was a town lady to me. We moved into the Charters' two-story log house on the ranch when I was just a baby, and she herself moved into a new house in Jackson, more than five miles away. Her house in town was modern and relatively fancy, located in a nice neighborhood that was fairly close to the town's shops, restaurants, and its one movie theater. I envied her all of this. I was conscious of the fact, from the time I was very small, that we were living in my great-grandmother's old house, which had been the Charters' house, on the Charter Place, and I thought it was too bad that so many things in my life, including the house we lived in, were hand-me-downs. I had a high opinion of new things and we didn't seem to have many.

Although I thought of her as a town lady, I eventually did learn a little about Sylvia's pioneer heritage and some of the details of her life before I came along. It turned out that Sylvia had actually written an autobiography when she was in her eighties, and when I expressed curiosity about her a few years before Granddad's death, he produced it for me. (I'm still haunted by the idea that he wouldn't have produced it for me if I hadn't asked, especially after having read it.)

Sylvia Irene Wood had been the sixth of eleven children, though the youngest three did not survive beyond early childhood. When she was seven years old her family moved from Utah to Star Valley, Wyoming, not far from Jackson Hole.

"Father fed cattle there, and in his spare time he dried deer meat," she recounted. "In Star Valley, Father took up some land at Auburn where we lived in an old log house with three rooms (we kids slept three in a bed). In the summer the boys slept out in a shed. Mother sewed rags together and made a carpet, under which was placed straw to make it wear longer. Muslin covered the ceiling and was taken down once a year to be washed. In one corner of the room our flour supply was stacked high.

"In the fall Father and the boys went to Eagle Rock (now Idaho Falls, Idaho) and picked potatoes, then brought back our winter supply of food and clothes. Mother gave Father a list of yardages of cloth, buttons, thread, etc., needed for dresses for each of us, as well as shirts for the boys, and Father picked out all of the materials. Then Mother made them up. His selections were very good, and one dress I got was made from a black material with a little rosebud in it, and I almost felt like a queen when wearing it. One time he brought me home a pair of shoes with both shoes for the same foot. Needless to say, a trip back to town was out of the question, so there was nothing to do but wear them. I can remember standing in church or some other public place trying to keep one foot hidden behind the other so people wouldn't notice."

But most of her memories of childhood do not convey hardship. "On warm summer evenings," she wrote in one captivating paragraph, "we went to the field near the house to play with June bugs. We would collect a dozen or more of the bugs which were about one inch long and one-half-inch wide, and dark brown with hard wings over their backs. We pretended that they were our horses and we would herd them into different corrals that we had made from sticks.

"They never attempted to fly," she took care to add, "but always crawled slowly."

When she was still a young girl, Sylvia's mother died, and she was compelled by her circumstances to become an adult, though in some ways, with her responsibilities of caring for the younger children, she already was one. She wrote, "Mother was sick all the month of February. I cared for Elva, who was four, and always had charge of her. Mother lost another baby—a girl who was named Isabelle. After that Mother was very ill. One afternoon she called us children all to her bedside and told us good-bye. She kissed us and said, 'Sylvia, be a good girl.' She died February 28, 1895. I cannot remember Elva crying for Mother afterwards, as she was always content to be with me. I was nine years old."

Sylvia's father remarried rather quickly, and from her description the family struggled somewhat to get along. Then as a young teenager Sylvia moved in with another family to work as a nanny, and finally, at their urging, completed an eighth-grade education. At that point she was able to get a teaching certificate for third grade, and the Idaho superintendent of schools gave her a three-month assignment at a school on Cedar Creek, a tiny community about sixteen miles above Blackfoot, Idaho. A cattleman named Peter (also known as P.C.) Hansen was sent to fetch her and bring her to the school.

"I received $45 a month," she wrote, "and when the three months were up, the two families said if I would teach for two more months, they would let me pick two yearling heifers from their cattle for my pay. This I did—except that Peter picked them out for me." Their friendship had thus begun.

Their courtship, according to Sylvia, reached its culmination in a creek bed. "One time when Peter was there and was ready to go home, he was breaking a colt and said, 'Get in and I'll take you for a short ride,' so I hopped in. The colt wouldn't turn and ran straight to the creek. The buggy tipped over and we were piled out."

"That's a sure sign Pete will marry Wood," remarked a neighbor, according to Sylvia. She didn't explain why such an occurrence would've been a predictor of marriage—perhaps it was the fact that Peter and Sylvia could get into a such a wreck together and walk away unharmed—but it was. And in 1906, when Sylvia was twenty-one and Peter was thirty-nine, they wed. In Sylvia's autobiography she included not only the story of their courtship but also of the wedding itself, along with a word-for-word transcript of the short article that was published about their wedding in the Blackfoot, Idaho, newspaper.

Her groom, Peter Christofferson Hansen, recounted the occasion in considerably less detail. He also wrote an autobiography, but when you read it you get the impression that it wasn't his own idea to write things down. He devoted a total of seven pages to his remarkable life story. His courtship of Sylvia, and their eventual marriage, is covered in the middle of one paragraph about the cattle business in the following single sentence: "Spring of 1906 I married, moved to the ranch west of the Snake River, got a hay job from Andy Mattson."

P.C.'s autobiography is mostly about land and cattle, not personal stories about himself or other people, even those most dear to him. P.C. died nearly a decade before I was born, so for most of my life I knew only what others told me. There are two principal anecdotes that his son, my grandfather Clifford Hansen, would often repeat about him. The one that first stuck with me was that his father was believed to have crossed the Snake River on horseback more than any other person living or dead.

I've never crossed the Snake River on horseback myself. The riverbed is lined with big, round, tumbled rocks, and in most places it would not be that easy for a horse to keep his footing, even in low water. In the spring runoff it wouldn't be long before your horse had no footing, and you might both be carried swiftly down the river for quite a ways before you could propel yourself to the other bank. But for some time, although he was living at his original homestead on the west side of the river, my great-grandfather was acquiring land on the east side. Keeping both places irrigated in the summer and the cattle fed on both places during the winter meant crossing the river every day. In high water it was a hair-raising swim, and in winter it was near freezing. According to Granddad, "One time he got in swimming water and he was swept away from his horse, but he managed to grab the horse's tail and he held on for dear life. So when he got to the other side he was with his horse."

"Which was fortunate," Granddad felt it necessary, after a pause, to inform me. "You don't relish being on foot all that much."

My uncle Peter, my mom's only sibling, tells that story differently. He says his father's father lost his grip on the tail, never did catch up with his horse, and had to walk the several miles home through the snow in his wet clothes—the remarkable thing being that his wide pant legs froze into casings like stovepipes, and although he had to walk rather stiffly, he was amazed that his legs warmed up inside their carapaces and he was quite comfortable.

I suspect my uncle's account is correct or that maybe both stories are true and happened at different times. The story is not recounted in P.C.'s own rather stunted biography. But it doesn't matter, because each version is worth remembering, in our family, and repeating. In Granddad's mind it just went to show that it's always best to be with your horse and worth doing whatever's necessary to stick with him. Uncle Peter's version, where things aren't always as bad as they might initially seem, is equally instructive.

Either way, Granddad's father eventually decided to consolidate his holdings on the east side of the Snake, so he no longer had to ford the river every day. Nonetheless, the image of him riding and sometimes swimming on horseback back and forth, back and forth, across the broad and deep Snake River has always defined the man for me.

The second tale that's often repeated about my great-grandfather is about how he was maimed while digging a grave for a little girl. The fact that my great-grandfather and another man were out digging a grave for the young daughter of a neighbor creates in my mind a bleak backdrop to the lives of my ancestors: how merciless life was in Wyoming, how much work those previous generations did to make it easier on the rest of us, how bitter the endings could be. The ground was hard and they were going at it with pickaxes when a rock chip flew up and hit Peter just above his right brow. He bled profusely, but rather than quitting the job which no one took pleasure in, he dabbed the wound with the dirty handkerchief of the man with him. From that he contracted erysipelas, an acute streptococcus bacterial infection, a condition that nearly cost him his life and did cost him his eye. Much later he was able to go to Chicago to be fitted with an artificial eye to wear.

This is the one personal anecdote that is recounted in P.C.'s autobiography, and he added these details to the incident:

The next day I was quite ill—grew worse and infection set in. John Miller (my neighbor) had a daughter, Mrs. Lewis, a trained nurse married to a doctor in Chicago, who was visiting here. She took care of me in the Miller home. She knew I would never get well if I didn't have my eye taken out, as I had developed erysipelas. My father and sister came in from Idaho. They called the doctor from Jackson, who was quite frequently drunk, and when he came in Mrs. Lewis grabbed his instruments and said, 'I'll sterilize these for you.' He said, 'Oh, I always keep them clean.' She sterilized them anyway and the operation was performed. Still I grew worse and medicine had to be sent from Rexburg [Idaho]. Horses were stationed along the way so a fresh horse could be picked up and a rider got here in time with the medicine *to save my life. . . . [S]everal months passed by before I could work again, and it cost me $1,300.*

For him even this episode, where "the operation was performed" that took from him his right eye, came down to how it affected his fortunes in the cattle business. Most all of his autobiography has to do with how much he paid for land or cattle, or how much he sold them for, or how much the cattle weighed, or who he bought them from. His attention to business accounts for how our family came by all our property. I knew that my great-grandparents, like so many early Jackson settlers, had been homesteaders, but it wasn't possible to homestead thousands of acres. They'd purchased it.

As a young man, P.C. worked in lumber camps. During their business careers his parents had owned both sheep and cattle. One year P.C. and his brother bought some cattle from their father when prices were fairly high, and when it came time to sell them in the fall, the market had dropped so low they couldn't get enough money out of them to even repay the debt they owed their father. P.C.'s brother had a family to support so he had to get a job. But P.C. kept the cattle and wintered them over on the Snake River bottoms near Fort Hall, Idaho.

P.C. slept in a tepee all winter, according to Granddad, and before retiring for the night he would prepare fuel so he could have a little heat as he was dressing the next morning. The only way to feed the cattle was to ride his horse in circles all day, breaking trail through the snow. The horse's hooves pulled the long tufts of slough grass up through to where the cows could get at it and survive. But the cattle market did not recover that year, or the next. Ultimately it took three years before my great-grandfather was able to finally sell the cows for what he owed and break even.

At the time P.C. thought he'd used up three years of his life with nothing to show for it, but the story of the way he'd nursed the cows through those harsh winters at Fort Hall, living in a tepee, became well-known in the area. And the credit P.C. gained—the fact that others knew he could be taken at his very word—is what enabled him in the coming decades to make significant purchases of both real estate and cattle. When he moved to the northern part of Spring Gulch Road in Jackson Hole and started buying property, the Standard Bank of Blackfoot, Idaho, told him, "Buy anything you want. Write a check and we'll cover it."

Although P.C. talked more about the cattle business than anything else in his short autobiography, he didn't actually cover how he'd prevailed through the Fort Hall winters, or the fact that this was how he'd established his credit and later, built his holdings. Perhaps he didn't want to make himself sound too grandiose, or maybe he didn't think what he'd done was out of the ordinary.

Granddad, P.C.'s son, was the one who related the Fort Hall story to me, but not until he was in his mid-nineties. I'd asked him to tell me about his life, and, in particular, his early years. He, too, was reluctant to recount his success, either as governor or as a US senator, and spent most of the time talking about his mother and father. As he neared the end of his life he seemed to reflect more on his parents' lives than his own, even in our more casual conversations. He spoke often of the accomplishments of his mother and father, and saw them as epic. As he described it, his parents' capacity for work had no apparent limits. Their willingness to keep at it despite setbacks and hardships—the illnesses and injuries that befell both them and their children, intermittent troubles with Indians and outlaws, a climate that sometimes brought debilitating and deadly snowstorms—verged on the heroic, something that could never be adequately commended.

And at least in the case of Granddad's father, it hadn't been commended in even the usual and customary way, because after his death there'd been no eulogy at his brief funeral.

When P.C. Hansen died rather suddenly of cancer in 1952, Sylvia was in Denver, attending to medical problems of her own. Everyone assumed there would be a planned memorial service at some point when Sylvia had returned, and that P.C. would be properly remembered, so they didn't worry about the brevity of the proceedings held at the little log Episcopal church in town. But after it was over, a ranching neighbor confronted Granddad on their way out of church.

"Why didn't you say something about your dad?" he asked.

My grandfather never forgave himself. He saw this as a personal failing from that day forward, particularly since the proper memorial service never ended up happening, and when we talked about his father, Granddad lamented the unwritten eulogy to me more than once.

There aren't many pictures of P.C., but my mother long ago gave me one of him taken with the family. Thus, I always picture P.C. Hansen as a man of sixty-eight, his age when the photo was taken. In the photo he is not a large man (which came as a surprise to me), and he doesn't have much hair across his pale head. He is darkly tanned from the eyebrows down, and wears a crinkled smile. The photo includes most of P.C. and Sylvia's children, including my grandfather and grandmother, and even my mother, though she's just a newborn in Granddad's arms.

There are more pictures of my great-grandmother Sylvia, including a well-known one that I've seen in books about Jackson history, as well as on the wall of a sourdough restaurant that used to be in town. In this photo she's washing dishes out in the middle of a sagebrush flat with my grandfather when he was a boy. He is holding the dishtowel and drying what looks like a tin plate. This picture has been reprinted several times in an effort to convey the rather harsh conditions that were endured by early Jackson pioneers, and indeed, Granddad told me he'd been very perturbed that day, but not for lack of a kitchen. He was not old enough to be riding with the cowboys and moving the herd as his older sisters were, and he had been left at the wagon to do the dishes with his mother.

But the great-grandmother I knew when I was growing up no longer had to wash dishes in the sagebrush, and she'd come a long way from the afternoon when her groom-to-be upended their buggy in the ditch.

I remember her as elegant and beautiful, even sophisticated. She almost always wore a dress and high-heeled shoes with seamed hosiery, and she wore her hair up. She had grayish-white hair all the way down her back and she wove it into a single braid, then wound the braid up in concentric circles on the back of her head and secured it there with hairpins. At the time I thought this was the most beautiful way a woman's hair could be done. But refined as she was, she always had a tough pragmatism to her just like any Wyoming pioneer woman. If you expected to get along in northern Wyoming at the beginning of the century as she had done, I suppose pragmatism would have been the minimum requirement. And that characteristic continued to serve and define her even when she was living a life of relative ease in town.

I saw her demonstrate that when I was about six years old and we caught a mouse in a spring-loaded trap in the kitchen of the house at the Bar Double R, a ranch we had that was located about twenty miles east of Jackson. Granddad, together with his sisters Parthenia and Geraldine, had purchased the Bar Double R in the late 1950s. It had been built up by a woman Granddad referred to as Mrs. McCormick, whose father had owned the *Chicago Tribune*. Mrs. McCormick had owned the Bar Double R primarily for the personal enjoyment of herself and her friends, but my great-aunts and grandfather bought it for the summer pasture as much as for its natural beauty. It was only a summer ranch because it was not accessible in the winter except by horseback, and later on, snowmobiles.

As for the hapless mouse, we had him that afternoon merely by the end of his tail. As the poor creature skittered around the kitchen with the wooden trap flapping behind, Sylvia hopped after it, stomping with the pointy heel of the fancy shoe on her right foot. I don't know if she managed to impale the mouse on her heel or not because I escaped out the back door, horrified, yet at the same time deeply impressed.

It was an oddity at the time to see a beautiful older woman in a tailored dress, silk hose, and high heels, hopping in deadly pursuit of a rodent, but I could see that my elegant great-grandmother had a steely nerve. It might not have been such an oddity if I'd known more about how she'd grown up—if I'd known about the straw-stuffed rag carpeting, or the cooperative little June bugs of her childhood.

I knew a bit more about Granddad's early years, most of which I'd learned from my mother, but some that—even though he preferred to talk about his parents—I eventually drew out of him.

Granddad was the third of P.C. and Sylvia's six children, all of whom grew up doing ranch work: herding cattle, building fences, clearing sagebrush, doctoring calves, putting up hay. Of course my grandfather grew up to be a skilled cowboy, but he often mentioned the great regard he had for his two older sisters, Parthenia and Geraldine, and their abilities with cattle, horses, and firearms, among other things.

P.C. had given Geraldine a small pistol when she was a girl, said Granddad. When he talked about this in his late nineties, he still smiled and shook his head in admiration at what a crack shot she was. Their mother Sylvia would send Gerry out to get a chicken for supper, he recalled, and she could shoot one right through its bobbing head with her little pistol from quite a distance away.

There was a respite from working the land and cattle when they were in school. Granddad, like his siblings, was a hard worker both on the ranch and in the classroom, but he was actually sent home from school when he was a little boy, bearing a note from the teacher for his mother to read. The note instructed Sylvia not to send little Cliff back to school—that he was, according to her, "uneducable."

The teacher didn't even think Granddad was capable of reading the note, but in fact he'd read it as soon as he'd left the schoolroom, and he had to walk all the way back to the ranch with it pinned to the front of his shirt. His problem was simple: He stuttered terribly, to the point where he was afraid to speak at all, and he couldn't manage to communicate to his teacher either how much he was learning or how much he already knew. But he was perhaps used to being underestimated by then.

He happened to be walking past the bunkhouse windows one day when he overheard a few of the ranch hands laughing about his halting efforts to form words and sentences. The ranch hands, "meaning no harm," according to my grandfather, were imitating him, joking that he'd probably do quite well, that he'd probably be "g-g-governor one day." How much that had to do with Granddad's ultimately pursuing and achieving the office of governor I do not know, but in any case, his mother, who'd been a schoolteacher herself, defied the teacher and made sure Cliff got an education. Eventually he was able to overcome his speech impediment with the help of a special school. He told it this way:

My parents read an advertisement by the Benjamin N. Bogue Institute in Indianapolis, Indiana, guaranteeing its ability to overcome this speech handicap. Following the beef roundup on the north Fish Creek Range of the Teton Forest, our cattle, along with those of our neighbor, Bert Charter, were driven to the George Cross Ranch near Dubois, Wyoming, where Walter Knollenberg of Tipperary was employed to guide the trail herd to Hudson, Wyoming. From there our cattle, along with those of Mr. Charter's, were loaded on railroad cars at Hudson, destined for Omaha, Nebraska, a major livestock marketing center. Despite my age as a young teenager, along with my father I began the journey to the Bogue Institute. My father accompanied me all the way to Indianapolis by train. He left me there and they worked with me for several weeks and it made a tremendous difference to me.

I repeat that story in Granddad's exact words because when Granddad wrote it down for me, eighty years after the events actually took place, I was struck by how this monumental turning point in Granddad's life, the way he told it, was more about the many particulars of how they got the cattle to market—with the first 135 miles of it on horseback—than it was about what had happened to him.

My grandmother Martha did not grow up in the cattle business. She grew up in Sheridan, Wyoming, which by Wyoming standards was a good-size metropolis, and she met Granddad at the University of Wyoming. According to Martha, her mother and father were quite concerned when she announced she wanted to marry a rancher from Jackson Hole, which was known as a rough outpost. And in fact her father remarked, prior to meeting Granddad in person, that to the best of his knowledge there was nothing but horse thieves and outlaws in Jackson Hole.

Of course they got married anyway, but during the early years of their marriage the circumstances were not cushy. Grammy and Granddad could not afford a house of their own so they lived in the bunkhouse, next door to Granddad's parents. My grandmother had two babies before long, my mother and my uncle, Peter, and they all lived together in the small, two-story bunkhouse, she with her husband, son, and daughter on the main floor, and the ranch hands upstairs. When I asked her how she managed it, living in the bunkhouse with the ranch hands as a young wife with two small children, she answered only that, "They were all nice men."

Eventually, of course, Grammy went from the bunkhouse to her own house, and then from frontier wife to first lady, and her surroundings over the years became quite a bit more comfortable.

By the time Granddad decided to run for governor in 1962, he was a fairly well-known person by Wyoming standards, partly because he'd headed the University of Wyoming board of trustees, and partly because he'd been president of the state Stock Growers Association. The Stock Growers Association was started among Wyoming cattle ranchers to standardize and organize the cattle industry, as well as to try and curtail the activities of cattle rustlers who plagued the West at that time. But the Association quickly grew into a political force that amounted to the de facto territorial government as Wyoming transitioned into statehood, because it was one of the few organizations that wielded any type of authority in the region.

Many years had passed since the Association had exerted this level of influence, but it was still a powerful organization when Granddad was leading it, and the experience was still relevant. Granddad wanted the state and its people to prosper, and whether it was through his own line of work or through public service, he thought he could help see to that.

People in Wyoming respected Granddad as a successful cattleman, and the more they got to know him and his wife, Martha, the more they liked them, too. Wyoming elections, then and now, are won or lost in trailer parks, high school auditoriums, and county fairs, not on television. Even today there is no Wyoming television station that is viewed statewide, so most people in Wyoming watch programming that originates in Utah or Colorado, which is one reason Wyoming politicking still has more to do with driving the highways and walking the neighborhoods than with buying media.

So my grandparents drove the highways and walked the neighborhoods, and they converted most people who met them in person and many by word of mouth. Granddad won the governor's race in the fall of 1962, and he and my grandmother moved the following January to

Cheyenne, leaving the ranch to the care of Mary and Pete. After four years in the governor's office Granddad decided to run for the US Senate. The work ethic and fair-mindedness that he'd brought to cattle ranching had served him well as governor, and he'd been liked and respected by people from both political parties. He succeeded in his bid for the Senate as well, and all in all, it was twenty years before he came back home.

I was just a toddler when Granddad was first elected, and by the time he retired from politics I was in college, so Grammy and Granddad weren't on the ranch that much during the years that I was. They lived in Cheyenne and then in Washington, and had what seemed to me to be innumerable luxuries.

Even in Wyoming the governor's mansion, built in a Colonial Revival style in 1905, was a stately and beautiful building, and Grammy and Granddad's life seemed to match it. We visited them at the governor's mansion in Cheyenne several times, and I saw the beautiful, formal rooms, the maids in uniform, the dresses my grandmother wore. I have a number of her gowns in my possession, and even now I'm amazed at their richness—the beadwork in gold and silver, the heaviness of the ivory silk underneath. Many of them were sleeveless, and she wore those with full-length kid gloves and pearls for State occasions. But even her everyday dresses during the political years were crisp and tailored, worn with hosiery and heels, not the cottony or woolly attire of the frontier wife that she'd been and, at heart, still was.

Though we didn't get to visit them in Washington that often, I did see their pictures in the paper from time to time as I grew up, and both of them always looked utterly elegant, quite far removed from the life I was living.

A life which I believed, because I knew then essentially none of the family history I've just related, was quite rustic.

4

Houses, Barns, and a Hole in the Ground

MUCH OF WHAT MADE MY LIFE A BIT TOO RUSTIC FOR MY TASTE HAD TO do with the ranch buildings. Sylvia's log house—the old Charter house, which became our house—wasn't the only old building on the Lower Ranch. All of the buildings were old. The cow barn and the horse barn, separated by a large rectangular corral, towered over the other structures just southwest of our house, across a short expanse of dirt yard. The first stories of both barns were constructed of logs, and the plank siding on the second stories didn't look as though it had been stained or painted at any point in time.

My grandparents had actually built a new house for themselves in the 1950s so that was relatively new, but it was not quite in the same orbit as the numerous other ranch buildings because it was set off by itself a hundred yards to the south of the main gate. It had its own driveway out onto Spring Gulch Road, and their yard had big trees all around the perimeter, part of the reason it didn't blend in with the rest of the ranch compound. Also, they didn't have any "working" buildings over there. No sheds, no equipment, and no junk. I didn't spend much time at my grandparents' house anyway, because, since they were in politics, they didn't live there most of the time. For me it existed where they existed: on a higher plane.

To the east of our house was a horse pasture, and from there you could see Spring Gulch Road winding up alongside the bottom of East Gros Ventre Butte. Our clothesline was just on the northeast side of the house, exposed to the road, and I was unsure if the way Mary hung our laundry out on the wires, where everyone driving up and down Spring

Gulch Road could see it, was really a good idea. Bedsheets, T-shirts, and even our underwear, just flapping in the breeze, even though there was a perfectly good dryer in the laundry room. I was embarrassed—not only because people could see our clothes, but because I was afraid they'd think we had no appliances. When I went out to gather laundry off the line I'd always make sure and put the hanging garments between myself and the road so the few passersby couldn't see me. I knew my mother didn't care about creating or avoiding any particular impression among the travelers on Spring Gulch Road herself; she simply preferred air-dried clothing.

Right across the lawn from our house to the west sat a bunkhouse and cookhouse, both constructed of ancient heavy logs, darkened with creosote and even older than our house, each settled into solidity if not quite level. The bunkhouse was pretty much off limits to me but I did enjoy the cookhouse. The kitchen in the cookhouse was one of the liveliest places to be because cooking—if you counted the preparations and the aftermath—had almost no end. Most of the year, there were half a dozen hands to feed three meals a day to—and during haying season, we could have as many as fifteen hands.

The cookhouse was not just where the cook lived, preparing and serving meals at the long table, but it was also a factory, to a certain extent. We had an amazing machine there called a separator, so large that it took up the entire anteroom next to the cookhouse kitchen. Our cook would take buckets of fresh milk, still warm out of the cow and usually with bits of grass, dirt, or manure floating in them, and pour the contents into a large funnel at the top of the separator. If you were in the room when this contraption was turned on you vibrated along with it and couldn't have a conversation with the person next to you for all the noise. With the use of centrifugal force it separated the cream, molecularly less dense, from the milk, and you could dial it up to where the milk had zero fat and the cream was so thick it wouldn't pour.

This thick cream was one of the few things we had in my childhood that I believed was superior to what other people had, and I still think that's true. In fact, I would be surprised if this kind of cream still exists in the world today. Maybe there's a lovely Jersey cow somewhere that's as nice as the one we named Posy; maybe she gives off a rich, sweet kind of milk like Posy's, and maybe somebody still has an old-fashioned separator that produces cream so high in fat you have to spoon it—cream that doesn't even melt on a hot pancake, which was my favorite way of eating it—but I would be surprised. I suspect the cream I'm speaking of is lost to the world, and maybe people other than my brothers and me and a handful of ranch hands wouldn't remember it ever existed.

Some of our early cooks made butter from the cow's milk, hand-churning it with wooden paddles in a gallon jar and then forming the solids into thick slabs which were wrapped into neat packages with waxed paper. My memories of the butter are not as keen as my memories of the cream, though, because I was pretty young when it became economically acceptable for our cooks to buy butter. But I do remember that the color of the butter varied with the seasons; sometimes it was deep yellow, and sometimes nearly white. And likewise, the flavor of the milk and cream varied with the seasons, depending on what the cows were eating at the time. I didn't like drinking our milk when the stinkweed was in bloom in early spring, and I now know that stinkweed has not just an unlovely nickname but unsuitable genes, that it is a relative of mustard, and "a mustard bouquet" would be a good description of the milk I didn't like.

We didn't always have enough in the way of hired hands to use up all the milk we got, because the population of hands also fluctuated with the seasons. The dairy cows had to be milked whether we needed the milk or not, however, and when there was a surplus it didn't make it as far as the separator. It was simply sloshed out into the usually dry ditch between the cookhouse and the vehicle sheds, where I had to walk right past it and, depending on how sunny and warm the weather had been, hold my nose.

But spoiled milk didn't bother me that much. We didn't pasteurize or homogenize our milk, so it spoiled pretty quickly. In fact, I was already in junior high by the time it occurred to me that the sour cream you could purchase in a store was in any way related to the sour cream I might find sitting in a glass bowl in our refrigerator, which was just regular cream that had gone south. I was intrigued the first time I tried commercial sour cream. It was so white. So strangely consistent, too—no grayish water at the bottom, no clots. It didn't take me long to decide I liked it, because unlike the ranch sour cream, you could actually eat it plain.

But the ranch sour cream, the spoiled cream, was the basis for all of my mother's cakes. I've tried using store-bought sour cream to make cakes with my mother's recipes and they've come out dry and bland. For my mother's cake recipes, commercial sour cream does not do, and so her cakes are like Posy's cream—lost to mankind.

Other than the separator, the machine in the cookhouse that most intrigued me was the meat grinder. You could put just about anything through it short of a hip bone. We had a cook named Mimi for several years with whom I was close, and she sometimes let me stand on a stool and push the meat down into the grinder while she cranked the handle.

Mimi was perhaps five feet tall, sparely built, and I look back now and wonder how she cranked the handle of the big meat grinder around when there was a big slab going through it. "Watch your fingers!" she'd cry in her tiny voice, leveraging her small body's weight against the crank, and I followed her orders. The meat grinder seemed stout enough that I figured if I got my fingers down in there, my whole body would probably follow and be drawn all the way through if Mimi didn't stop cranking with both hands.

Mimi was someone my mother considered to be a great cook, although I later came to understand that "great cook" by Mary's standards meant someone who could plan, prepare, and clear away three nutritious meals a day, seven days a week, week after week after week. And these weren't just any meals. They weren't sandwiches. They had to be hearty enough to keep a crew of ranch hands going, even when the ranch hands were expending five thousand calories a day pitching hay.

Other people's ideas (including my own) about what constituted great cooking did not necessarily hold water with Mary. I marveled out loud one Thanksgiving about the immense French copper skillet—honestly, I think it was two feet wide—that a friend of ours had brought over with her contribution to the holiday dinner. In the circle of this shallow skillet the friend, who was truly a gourmet cook, had arranged vegetables in, of all things, a symmetrical mosaic: triangles of bright green peas, separated by lines of julienned carrots, with a border of glistening sautéed wild mushrooms around the outside. I thought this was fantastic, and I kept prodding my mother to join in my exclamations. She was grateful for the delicious vegetables, but I noticed that she did not quite share my enthusiasm.

"Look at these vegetables!" I said. "Can you believe how beautiful they are?" I went on, and my mother agreed, but in a way that would have to be classified as dutiful. Yes, the vegetables were amazingly pretty, she concurred. Even I could see that the beauty would only last as long as the vegetables remained undisturbed in the pan, but that didn't take anything away from them in my mind. Mary, of course, interpreted correctly that I was curious about why she never made anything as wonderful as this giant skillet of arranged vegetables.

She had a similar reaction when I came home from my piano lesson in town one afternoon and started going on about all the horse ribbons my piano teacher had won. I'd been somewhat dazzled, because even though my piano teacher had only one horse (while we had a pretty good-size herd out in the pasture), she had nonetheless managed to accumulate a whole wall's worth of awards.

"She must be a fantastic horsewoman," I told my mother. "She has a collection of ribbons she's won that covers a whole entire wall in her house." Mary was politely impressed, but I could tell she was holding back. "Don't you think that's great?" I asked. "That she's won so many awards for horse riding?" For all I knew my mother had horse ribbons, too, but I'd never seen any.

Mary was not willing to say anything about it beyond "Good for her," which seemed like deliberately lukewarm praise. She didn't explain, but I knew my mother well enough by then to know that it wasn't an issue of envy. It was just that, as much as I might've wanted it to be, a wall of ribbons wasn't the real world from Mary's perspective, any more than the gourmet cook's beautiful mosaic of vegetables was the real world. Mary was running a cattle ranch, and in her world, no one was handing out ribbons, and Mimi was a great cook.

In any case, mealtime at the cookhouse was not designed to be a source of wonderment or surprise for anyone; it was designed to be a source of replenishment and fuel for ranch hands, so you didn't necessarily need a large repertoire and you could never go wrong with meat and potatoes. Foreign dishes would have included spaghetti and Swiss steak and that's about it.

We had quite a few cooks come and go when I was growing up on the ranch, but Mimi had a fairly long tenure. She came to us because her daughter had been married to my uncle Peter, and she was the grandmother of my cousins. She treated us like we were her grandchildren, too, and before I was school age, I often went to the cookhouse to play when it was cold outside. She had a woodstove right in her kitchen and a wide selection of things to play with, including the big butter churn, some very large mixing bowls, and a heavy wooden rolling pin. She'd get them all out and put them on the floor for me to fiddle with, and before I became jaded about the idea of playing with things like butter churns, I thought it was much more fun and interesting than anything we had at our house.

My mother had a meat grinder at our house, too, and she used it the same way Mimi did, but it wasn't as big as the one at the cookhouse. Mary used the grinder for cooked meat more than for raw, because it allowed you to use up leftovers by making them into hash. Mary did not advocate wasting things—not food in general, and certainly not meat.

Steaks, hamburgers, roasts, pork chops, even bacon—almost any kind of cooked meat could be put through the grinder, followed by an onion and some boiled potato. All of this would be molded into a loaf of hash to be cooked again and served doused with ketchup, lest you choke on the inevitably arid mixture. The hired men could count on having hash every couple of weeks over at the cookhouse—with the copious quantities of food Mimi served, even they had leftovers—and our family was on about the same schedule. Although I liked the meat grinder I didn't enjoy hash, but then I was probably overfamiliar with the age and variety of the different items that had disappeared down the gullet of the grinder to create it.

Mary didn't really ask us for feedback on the subject of food. What we thought we liked or didn't like when it came to the menu was unnecessary input, and she didn't ask us what we might like for supper anyway, because, given how far away the grocery store was, she'd planned the supper menu a week in advance. So unless it was a special occasion we got what we got.

Some of what we got had to do with what was available at the small grocery store in town, which was about a hundred miles from the nearest place that had a growing season long enough to actually produce food. But sometimes the menu had to do with what was available on our own property. One day my father called Mary from the Double T to say a cow had died up there and they'd decided to go ahead and butcher it. An unplanned death was often how we came by beef for our own personal consumption; it wasn't as if we picked the best animal out of the herd and set it aside for ourselves. In fact, according to my grandfather, he didn't eat beef until he was in college at the University of Wyoming.

"Beef is what we produced," he clarified for a colleague after he was in politics. "We ate deer and elk."

The death of the cow at the Double T that day apparently called for quick action on my mother's part, and as soon as she hung up the phone she put on the rubber gloves she kept under the kitchen sink, grabbed a couple of plastic mop buckets, and headed for the door. "Come on, Muffy," she said, giving me one of the buckets to carry rather than an explanation of what it was we had to go and do. I took the bucket and got into the truck beside her with a certain squeamishness creeping up inside of me.

When we arrived at the Double T my father and a couple of the men had already succeeded in gutting the animal and were standing around next to the shed, apparently waiting on my mother's arrival. I wanted to know what had happened to the poor cow, whose carcass was lying off to the side, but I didn't ask, and nobody volunteered the information. Pete knew, Mary knew, and I didn't need to know, although it looked to me like its leg was broken.

Mary hopped out of the truck and, using both hands, plucked the animal's heart and liver from the gut pile, slopping each into its own mop bucket. I carried the heart and she carried the liver back to the truck, and we brought them home.

The liver was sliced and frozen, and we had stuffed heart for supper that night. Mary packed the ventricles—how handy they were—with seasoned bread stuffing before roasting it. At dinner we ate the thick, dark slices of heart; it was her own recipe, and one of my favorites. I didn't enjoy the heart any less than usual that evening but partly because of that day, thanks to Mary, I've felt clear ever since about where certain things come from, and what they are, and that you have to be okay with that—and grateful for it—or not eat them.

That all had to do with the cookhouse, more or less, but I was very familiar with all the buildings on the Lower Ranch. None of them were off limits (except for the bunkhouse in the interest of the hired men's privacy), and I went around as if all of the other buildings were an extension of our house and sometimes my own bedroom. I had numerous personal items such as books, hairbrushes, and play dishes stashed in various places around the ranch—not only in the little playhouse we had, but also in the cabinets of the sheep camp, in the cabs of unused vehicles, and in the scratchy places between stacked hay bales up in the hayloft.

My brothers and I spent quite a bit of our free time in the hayloft of the horse barn. We liked playing in the hayloft of the cow barn, too, but the horse barn was smaller, and you could actually jump down from the loft window out into the corral if somebody had happened to dump a load of dry manure from the cattle truck there for you to land on.

You had to be careful tromping around the hayloft of the horse barn, though, because there was a wide gap in the floor right above the horse stalls. This was so that hay could be easily sent down by the pitchfork-load into the mangers. We had installed a spare board about six inches wide in order to get from one side of this gap to the other and have the run of the whole loft.

I can visualize my little brother Matt, who at the age of two was an inexpert walker, attempting to get across the four- or five-foot length of that narrow bridge. I can't think how Brad and I, ages five and four at the time, got him up the wooden ladder to the hayloft in the first place, but I can still recall with great visual detail his short little legs in a snowsuit, swinging in a stubby stride across that board above the horse stalls, ten feet below. I watched from behind as, to my amazement, his tiny foot took that next step into the air and he was gone.

Brad and I retrieved Matt—by then a crumpled, crying heap—from the manger as soon as we could get ourselves down there, and brought him back to the house with blood running down his face. I was somewhat horrified at the amount of blood, but when we handed him over to my mother, she was inexplicably not all that horrified or mad at us, even though our little brother had broken his nose.

I often didn't understand Mary's system of thinking. She'd be upset with me for letting my right shoe—a pointy hand-me-down from my city-dwelling older cousin, a shoe which I never would've chosen, which was still too large, and, which was as far as I was concerned, already worn out—fall into the creek and go down the culvert, while sometimes letting the really big crimes go unpunished.

She had her own measuring stick for crime. For her, hoisting our little brother up the side of the barn to a place where he could fall and hurt himself was not actually a big crime on our part. It was something that, in fact, could be categorized as industry, which she encouraged. I believe the most egregious crime for Mary would have been laziness, and following that would probably have been carelessness and heedlessness (as in, "Oops, there goes my ugly shoe")—but only because they were closely related to laziness.

My father, too, was more apt to get upset about carelessness or laziness than about mistakes, especially when the mistakes were committed with rigorous effort. He could be very generous about cleaning up the messes our efforts sometimes came to, and, at times, he even abetted our schemes. When Brad and Matt and I decided one summer between junior high years that we wanted to build a secret underground fort, he took the backhoe over to the relatively flat ground at the bottom of the draw across from my grandparents' house and dug us a large, rectangular hole. Pete was a master with a backhoe, and I think if we'd asked him to, he could've dug a hole in the shape of a rabbit, but for our fort, a rectangle was what was called for, and when he was finished it had nice sharp corners, straight sides, and an even, flat floor.

When I say we decided to build an underground fort, I'm pretty sure that means Brad decided to. I often did what Brad wanted because I admired him, and Matt often did what I wanted because I bossed him. Thus, on many occasions we worked together toward a common goal.

With Pete's fresh-dug rectangle as our starting point Brad and Matt and I were consumed with vigorous toil, and went the rest of that day without food and water, dragging old lumber from the burn pile in the draw, piece by heavy piece, for our roof beams. We laid the poles and boards perpendicular to the beams across the hole, and found a few pieces of weathered, already-delaminating plywood to help seal it off. The final layer was just dirt, hard to shovel but easy to come by since there was at least half an acre at the bottom of the draw that had been scoured free of grass by the bulls, that being one of their gathering places.

Perhaps given the previous sentence you can see what's coming, but at the time Matt and Brad and I weren't thinking there could be any ill consequences, and my father, perhaps, had underestimated our camouflaging abilities.

We talked throughout the many grueling hours about how our heavy labor would be well worth it. For one thing, we imagined how scared our friends would be when, after one of us had somehow lured them to the draw, the others would suddenly appear out of nowhere. We also talked about living the rest of the summer in the hole, and discussed which table, chairs, and bookshelves we'd be bringing over from the house. After we'd put the last shovel full of dirt on top of our lumber ceiling we had to congratulate ourselves. No one would ever know it was there except for the small access hole we'd left at one corner. It was nearly dark, and we stumbled wearily as we made our way out of the draw and up the road to the house.

I went to bed that night the most dog-tired I'd ever been in my life. I fell backwards onto my unmade bed with my hands on the waist of my jeans; I didn't even have it in my power to get my pants off. I woke up the next morning with my feet on the floor, in the same position where exhaustion had felled me like a tree as I started getting ready for bed. I went down to breakfast to tell my mother how I'd slept with the unlikely idea that it would bring forth a glut of sympathy, but Brad, who'd gotten downstairs first, superseded that idea with the disappointing news he'd just learned from our father.

Apparently a big Hereford bull had wandered down through the draw for water in the night, oblivious to the peril of our underground fort. When he stepped on the disguised timber roof it had given way immediately, and he'd plummeted to the bottom of the big hole. He was trapped there as we spoke, bawling and considerably mad. Pete was about to go back over with the backhoe and get a rope around him to pull him out.

Our fort was ruined, and I was so upset I nearly started to cry, but not because I felt sorry for the bull who had gone into the abyss. As much as I liked cows, I knew that bulls could be mean. I never forgot the time Brad had been herding an old bull to the barn when it suddenly whirled, without any apparent reason other than being grouchy, and stuck its horn into the chest of Brad's horse. The horse stumbled and fell to the ground and was fortunate to survive, and that incident was one reason I didn't trust bulls and didn't like them.

On the other hand, I didn't blame them for their nature. I knew the cantankerous tendency of bulls was due mostly to the fact that we'd not removed their testicles. It was pretty plain evidence when you compared bulls to castrated steers that animal behavior was largely a product of chemistry and wiring. So I was begrudgingly happy to hear that the bull, after he was hoisted out of the debris of our underground fort, was still in one piece. But I was grief-stricken over the waste of our many hours of hard work, and the ruination of the fort we hadn't been able to enjoy for a single day.

I'd been too tired and disheartened even to go and watch Pete haul the bull out. My father ended up using the backhoe to carry all the lumber we'd brought from the burn pile back to where we'd found it, and then he filled in our hole, and that was the end of that. I don't know if I was grateful to Pete for cleaning up the lumber or if I ever said thank you, but what I do know is that the three of us weren't in any trouble. We'd made a giant mess of things and nearly broken the legs of a valuable bull (which would've ended his life), but we hadn't been lazy.

There were more than enough places on the ranch, however, for Brad and Matt and me to have forts and secret stashes without having to build, or dig, our own. On the far west end of the building envelope were a series of sheds, mostly used for parking idle equipment. These sheds seemed far away from our house, built as an afterthought, and because of their location behind the shop buildings they were cut off from most of the usual activity. Brad and Matt and I felt, because we hardly ever saw my parents or any ranch hands doing anything at the western-most sheds, that they were available for homesteading, and we built ourselves an elaborate fort in the rafters of one of these sheds.

Brad and Matt were fair at carpentry before we were out of grade school, and I was good at scavenging things from the plethora of items in storage. The finished fort had four distinct rooms, some of them with furniture, and we were certain that no adults were aware of its existence. We never installed a ladder or any easy way to get up there, in order to keep it a covert operation. You had to scale the log wall of the shed, and then when you got hold of the roof braces, hoist yourself up like a gymnast.

Most of the items we salvaged for that and other forts came from the old shop, which was my favorite building on the Lower Ranch, even more than the barns and maybe even more than the cookhouse.

I say "old shop" because when I was about thirteen we built a new shop with metal siding, all nice and clean with a concrete floor, a big roll-up door, and plenty of electrical outlets. At that time we'd stopped relying on draft horses to pull the hay wagon that fed the cattle in the winter, and instead had purchased a huge new tractor, one that wouldn't fit in our old shop. The new shop had a bigger footprint and higher ceilings, and my father could drive not only the new tractor in there but the backhoe, too, and it was a lot easier to work on the equipment when you could be inside next to your tools, warm and dry.

Although I was very much in favor of new buildings at the time, the new shop would never be as interesting as the old shop, because the old shop had been around long enough to accumulate a very wide selection of objects: antique tools, wartime pinup calendars, discarded welding projects, buckets of shiny black oil just begging to be stirred with a stick. Even more fascinating to me, the old shop also had a separate room, another log structure that had been tacked on to the north end of it at some point, which had accumulated an even wider selection of objects, some of which had been stored there for decades.

Like most descendants of homesteaders, our family was reluctant to throw things away, even items that were, to me, obviously used-up scraps. I recall how frustratingly slow it could be to simply walk, for instance, from our house past the gas pump and the horse barn to the old shop with my grandfather. When I was a teenager this was especially trying to me. Granddad lived in Washington at the time, not on the ranch, but even so, when he was home he was always stooping to pick up a bent nail or a scrap of wood or even a short length of baling twine, commenting as he went along on how easy it was to hammer a nail straight enough, and how this piece of wood was about the same size as the hole in the fence over there, and how often you might be grateful if you had a little baling twine in the glove box of your truck.

Many of the things we were reluctant to throw away ended up in the storage end of the old shop. Although I didn't appreciate the fact that we seemed to save every last kind of thing, I did find the contents of the storage building beguiling. Old newspapers, tires, furniture, discarded appliances, light fixtures, antlers, pieces of motors (or entire motors), and, most fascinating, bear bait.

I never knew exactly who in our employ hunted bears, and I don't remember anyone ever talking about having killed one. I do know that it wasn't unusual to lose a cow or two to bears during the summer as they grazed on the open range in Grand Teton National Forest, and I wouldn't have been upset about it if I knew someone who did lure and shoot a bear.

The bear bait was contained in a stash of random jars on the shelves at the far end of the old shop. Some of the jars were appropriate for canning beets and some were gallon-size, and they were all filled with putrid pieces of meat just rotting away behind the glass. Apparently it was important that the bear could smell the bait from a mile away. The pieces of meat in the bait jars didn't look like they'd ever been sirloin steaks, either. They were inedible organs, or maybe part of a tail, or some creature's brain or intestines.

That was the thing about the old shop: It was like a museum, but with a rather unspecific theme. If you poked around for a bit, you'd easily find a 1950s toaster or a wooden toilet seat or a lung in a jar.

I knew this partly because I became very familiar with the contents of the old shop one particular day after Mary had informed my brothers and me that there was just one other word in the English language that used the same letters as the word "chesty," and that we had one of these items in the old shop. She sometimes threw out little intellectual challenges, and this puzzle was like the time she announced she'd just bought "an anti-stratification device" for the family room, as she closed up the enormous Sears catalog that was the source of most of our household goods. I can't remember which one of us came up with "ceiling fan" first.

As for "chesty," I searched high and I searched low, my strategy being that coming upon the item would be a way around solving the word puzzle. I poked around for hours, climbing into the overhead shelves, and found myself rummaging through all kinds of oddities: cans full of grease, tools I couldn't identify, a large wall clock, tractor tires you could crawl inside of. I even sat down and read a Jackson newspaper because I noticed it had been issued in January of the year I was born, 1960, and I was fascinated to read in the birth announcements about the arrival of my friend Kathy.

I never did find a scythe but eventually I went back to the house and worked the problem out on paper and actually had it figured out before my brothers did.

The old shop was also where I learned to use power tools, although I never got to be as proficient as either Brad or Matt at most of them. I didn't learn how to weld until I was a teenager—not because I wasn't allowed to, but because I was afraid of the acetylene torch, and because the protective helmet and gloves were unwieldy. (When I finally did learn to weld, it was in high school shop class, not on the ranch. I had gotten a D in home economics earlier in my academic career and resented the fact that it was a required class for girls. I begged the principal to let me take shop instead, which he ultimately let me do, at which point I belatedly learned to weld.) But my brothers knew how to weld from an earlier age, and given the amount of scrap metal lying around, it was a skill worth knowing.

All three of us could use the drill press, grinder, soldering iron, and, of course, hammer and nails to build useful things for ourselves. We made rafts with which to navigate the creek, welded horseshoe nails into ninja stars, and ground scraps of metal into shivs. My parents didn't supervise or limit us in any noticeable way, although Pete got mad at us once for using up a stack of new lumber on a raft Brad wanted to build after reading *Kon-Tiki*. After that we made sure to steal only from the scrap pile, which wasn't that limiting, given the way our family saved everything.

As much as I admired the houses in town, especially the more modern ones, meaning those that weren't made of logs, I didn't envy the way most family homes involved just the one building. Which meant the people would be either inside their house, or outside their house, with no other places to go.

The Lower Ranch—with the horse barn, cow barn, cookhouse, bunkhouse, old shop, new shop, sheep camp, numerous equipment sheds, our own house, and even, if you wanted to venture into the outer orbit, my grandparents' house—had so many different places to explore, and they'd been constructed with such a variety of materials, including logs, planks, corrugated tin, wood shingles, and stone.

You could tell the ranch had been put together over a long period of time, and you could tell that the building skills, budgets, and availability of different materials had varied as the years went by. That it had so many different structures and had been created over the course of many years— this is what made the ranch feel almost like a small Western town.

But the other feature that made the ranch feel like its own little town was the number and variety of its inhabitants.

5

The Men

FROM THE TIME I WAS BORN I HAD THE COMPANY OF RANCH HANDS ON A near-daily basis. Some of them were employed for one haying season but some for half their lives, men and women who were usually somewhere within shouting distance when Brad and Matt and I played in the creek beds and haylofts, who rode with us when we herded cattle, and who often ate holiday meals at the dinner table in our home. Several of them, at different times, lived for years right across the yard from us in our log bunkhouse—room and board were part of their pay—and some of them were nearly like family to me.

In addition to our family of five we had a cook, and depending on the season, anywhere from half a dozen to perhaps fifteen ranch hands—more than two dozen if you counted those at the Double T and the Bar B C—all living in ranch buildings.

I refer to them now as ranch hands but that's not actually what we called them. We called them "the men," notwithstanding the fact that they were every now and then women. Those words, "the men," carried a lot of weight with me at the time. If Mary said, "Set the table for ten, Muffy; the men will be here for dinner," I would take the trouble to set the table correctly and fold the napkins with a sharp edge, because the men, the ranch hands, were held in high esteem.

I don't know if Pete and Mary treated their ranch employees differently than most other ranchers did, but I came to understand that how they operated wasn't typical of boss-employee relationships. Mary and I made a few visits to a friend of hers outside of Louisville after I was grown up, and her friend had a beautiful horse farm, classic Kentucky, with grounds and horses that were so well-kept they looked like part of a plastic play set to me, every green pasture framed in white-board fences that showed no signs of weather. Among the friend's employees was a housemaid, and when we visited, my mother would bring the maid a small gift and make a point of asking after her family members. I noticed that most of the other guests, gathered from various parts of the U.S. and Europe, were more mindful of the social barrier between server and servee, and it seemed like some of them wondered why my mother would breach what was to them a functional divide.

On our ranch it was functional to have the employees be on pretty equal footing with the bosses. My parents relied heavily upon the ranch hands and the decisions they made, and oftentimes hands worked alone, literally miles from anyone who might supervise them. Besides, when the workday was over, they lived next door.

One consequence of Mary and Pete's broad-mindedness was that we had many types of people with all kinds of different backgrounds and personalities who worked on the ranch over the years. Mary and Pete allowed their employees to do things their own way to a great extent. Working on the ranch was a different kind of job because ranch work wasn't just a job—it was a life, and many of the hands cared as much about the ranch as our own family did. It took a certain kind of person. Perhaps there aren't many of those types around anymore; you don't see a lot of people living in bunkhouses. Maybe there weren't even that many back then. But we always seemed to be able to find them when we needed them, or somehow, they found us.

Some of our ranch hands over the years had their idiosyncrasies, but if a person was willing to work hard, they could make a contribution that would be both valued and rewarded, to the sometimes-stretched ability of the ranch bank account to reward it. Pete and Mary's criteria seemed to be fairly simple and sensible.

I was fascinated by one particular crew-cut employee who chewed tobacco and used swear words and who I thought for sure was a man, but Brad said was really a woman. That Brad knew more fundamental things than I did was a given, but I thought I knew the difference between a man and a woman. I eventually noticed some of her telltale physical contours, and when I was finally introduced to her by name, discovered that Brad was right about her gender. In any case, what mattered to my parents was that this person could dig post holes and pitch hay, the kind of work a lot of people wouldn't be interested in, or good at, but she was.

We had a pair of brothers named Marty and Wayne who came over from their own ranch in Idaho every summer to help us mow our fields when the hay was high. They both had drinking problems, and eventually, according to my father, they drank their own place away. But Pete still had them come to mow our place after that because, even though they never got out from under the bottle, they did a thorough job of cutting the hay without tearing up the fields with their mower blades.

I picked up on the fact that my parents didn't look down on Marty and Wayne. Mary and Pete felt both sympathy for their problems, self-inflicted though they might have been, and admiration for their abilities, and made them part of the operation to the extent that it was beneficial to both sides. The younger brother Wayne actually got married to our cook right in our own pine-paneled living room one summer. My mother made all the arrangements and put on a nice reception for them, and had me wear my best dress. I don't think the marriage worked out because it wasn't too long before the cook was gone, and Wayne was still around, but Mary went to some effort for their wedding.

We had a ranch hand named Garcia for a while. I heard that he came from Mexico. I don't know how my parents found him, but I was extremely fond of him for the overriding reason that he brought my brothers and me candy. My mother hardly ever let us have candy, and in fact, I was so desperate for it before Garcia came along that I'd once stolen a roll of Lifesavers from Fred's Market, where we had a charge account and got all our groceries. I got them in my pocket when my mother wasn't looking and out of the store without anyone realizing it. It was a revelation to me—I thought I'd just discovered at the age of four how to get whatever I wanted. But as I worked my way through the Lifesavers I just flung the wrapper in numerous pieces under my bed where my mother shortly discovered them.

Mary knew I'd stolen the Lifesavers because until Garcia came to work for us, it was the only way I could've gotten my own candy. She wasn't at all angry with me. She simply had me take the house trash out to the fire barrels for a penny a trip until I had the money to pay back the grocery store, but that didn't take me very long, since at that time a roll of Lifesavers cost only five cents.

Earning the money wasn't the difficult part anyway. The difficult part was that Mary had me give the pennies to the checker at Fred's Market in person. Everyone knew everyone in Jackson so not only was I embarrassed by having to explain what I'd done to a familiar face at Fred's, but I also figured the story would be all over town by the time we got back to the ranch. It took me years to feel comfortable showing my face at Fred's again, but looking back, I don't imagine it was quite as much of a news flash as I believed. I only relate this story because it was so notable to me at the time when Garcia came along and used his own money to buy candy for Brad and Matt and me. Even though my mother didn't approve of too much candy, she did approve of Garcia, and she let him give it to us.

Garcia didn't stay with us for very long, and that turned out to be unfortunate. After he left our place he ended up getting arrested for killing another man in a knife fight. My father went all the way to Oregon to testify on behalf of his character at the trial, because Garcia had explained the circumstances to him and Pete said it was self-defense. But Garcia went to prison anyway. When Pete told Matt and Brad and me that Garcia wouldn't ever be coming back, it occurred to me that I didn't care about the candy after all; I just wished he could somehow get out of his punishment.

I never looked around when I was little and thought that I was lucky, or even that it was particularly interesting to be growing up in the company of so many different kinds of people. It was simply my world, and everything and everyone in it seemed to be a function of cattle ranching. I identified the different employees with the jobs they did, which was how we all did or didn't fit in. It was the ranch work that dictated everyone's presence and their purpose.

A man named Roy Schaple was one of the long-timers on our place, and I don't think he was known so much as a cowboy, but he was able to do many other kinds of jobs. He was sometimes a rather laid-back character, though, and could be seen gazing contentedly out the bunkhouse window for extended periods, even when the window he was looking out of faced nothing but the shed next door. Pete said he'd heard that Roy had run into some difficulties during his service in Korea, and that he might've received some treatment that affected his brain.

On a day when Roy was pretty late for lunch at the cookhouse, Pete went looking for him. He drove up the road toward the Bar B C, and just after he turned off onto the Bar B C lane, he spotted Roy's ranch truck, parked a little off to the side of the road, partially in the borrow pit and in the shade of some tall willow bushes. Mildly concerned, he pulled up alongside the truck and stopped so he could speak to Roy, who sat there in the driver's seat, smiling amiably at my father as he ground to a slow stop on the rough gravel of the lane.

Pete had to stretch across his pickup seat to roll down the window on the other side and talk with Roy, who was irrigating the hay ground at the Bar B C that summer. He was a hard worker, and he'd been working for our family, living in the bunkhouse, for the better part of ten years. Having room and board as part of your pay was a good arrangement for a bachelor such as Roy.

"Hello, Roy," said Pete, peering from across the seat. "What's the matter? You need some help?"

"Oh, no," replied Roy with a cheerful smile. "I'll get her going in five minutes or so."

"You sure? I can give you a ride if you're broken down."

"No, thanks." Roy arched the still-black eyebrows in his dark tanned face. He had kind of a small head and a sharp chin, and he raised his eyebrows while at the same time squinting his eyes when he smiled, and it gave him a look I always found congenial. "It's been quitting here every day, but it's not broke down. It'll get going in five minutes or so."

My father paused. "You say the truck quits in this same spot every day?"

"Yep," answered Roy. "It quits right about here, every day. Right when I'm on my way to lunch." He shook his head good-naturedly at the quirky disposition of the old truck. "But it'll start up again. I've just got to give it five minutes or so."

At that Roy seemed to be satisfied, but my father was not. He eased his truck ahead and off the road in front of Roy. When my father opened the door of his truck and got out, Roy apparently felt obliged to do the same, and gave my father a willing hand in getting the hood of the broken-down pickup unlatched and lifted.

Roy looked on with genuine curiosity as Pete checked the spark plugs, not surprised to discover that they were a little bit loose, and also wet. Roy had driven through a deep puddle about fifty yards back, a puddle created by the excess irrigation water that had flooded the adjacent fields and gullied over a low spot in the fence line onto the road.

The standing water had been on the road for several days, maybe a week, ever since Roy himself had irrigated that particular section of pasture. It was easy to picture Roy bouncing along the rough road to lunch at the middle of every day, his front tires smacking the puddle at full tilt and more than a few gallons of muddy water sloshing up through the engine block. The engine would die shortly thereafter, every time, but was only dead for the five minutes it took for the plugs to dry off. I suppose afterwards that Roy was happy to have the mystery of the truck's odd habits solved—as happy as you can be about getting the answer to a question you haven't asked.

My father told the whole story with all the details of their roadside conversation at supper that night, and retold it more than once in the years that followed, but when he repeated it, it was with fondness for Roy. And every time I heard it I enjoyed picturing Roy there, and even envied him, being neither inconvenienced nor troubled, accepting as a gift five minutes of solace on the side of a dirt road on a blithe summer day. That it kept happening might have made it all the more satisfying, for all I know.

Roy's contribution on the ranch wasn't always so passive, however, and didn't always go down so easily. I will never forget the time Roy had to shoot one of our horses in front of me. Mary and Pete had gone to a dinner party and left my brothers and myself, still in grade school, at home. We were rarely on the ranch alone. Sometimes we had babysitters, but almost any evening there would be ranch hands and the ranch cook right next door in the bunkhouse and cookhouse, respectively, and that evening, all the hands were home.

On this particular night, someone (probably me) had left the gate to the horse pasture open, and some of the horses, about ten of them, were milling around the lawn and wandering through my mother's garden. I say "probably me" because the gate to the horse pasture was not a swinging gate; it was a slack section of barbed-wire fence that, in order to close, you had to stretch tight to the end post until you could get a short loop of barbed wire over the gate pole. It was very difficult when I was little, and not that much easier when I grew up, to pick up a ten-foot section of fence which included three or four heavy stretcher poles and get it pulled far enough over to close the gap. And once I'd done that, standing there with all my weight leveraged to keep the gate tight, getting the loop on was often impossible. Of course, not being able to close a gate is one thing; walking away is another.

The horses couldn't have gotten out onto the road that evening because the main gate to the ranch was closed, and next to it was the cattle guard. But Brad and Matt and I didn't want Mary and Pete to think we couldn't manage the ranch while they were gone, so we determined that we ought to get the horses gathered up and moved back into the pasture before my parents got home.

We got on three sides of them and started hooting and hollering, with what in retrospect might've been too much bluster. Pretty soon we had them on the run, even though space was relatively tight in between the fences, sheds, barns, and the open pasture gate. In my memory they were headed right where we wanted them, their necks taut, heads high and ears back, flustered, I'm sure, at the hopping up and down and hollering of the three small persons at their flanks.

"Git!" I yelled, in a bossy voice. Perhaps my brothers were yelling too. At that, one horse broke from the rest and wheeled to the right, heading straight for the ranch entrance and the open road. I didn't run after him because I could see I couldn't get there fast enough to head him off. But for some reason, although the horse surely knew better, he loped right onto our metal cattle guard, and at once his slippery, shod hooves dropped between the rails and he fell down onto his belly with his legs dangling through, probably all the way to the standing water below. The rails of that cattle guard were not constructed as tubes, but were long, thin sheets of iron bent into squared-off, upside-down V's. I'd fallen into that cattle guard myself, and I knew the edges were sharp, so as the gelding struggled and whinnied I hoped he wasn't cutting his legs.

Brad by then had run to the bunkhouse for help. Roy and a few others came out and got the remaining horses settled in the pasture, then put a halter on the stuck horse. With two men pulling on the heavy halter rope, they managed to give the horse enough leverage so that he was finally able to clamber out.

But that was no relief to Brad, Matt, or me. We could see as the horse's hindquarters finally emerged from the metal rails that he'd shredded one of his hind legs below the hock. His hoof was no longer there, and his tendons and muscle fibers dangled freely, along with a strip of his sorrel hide. Roy led him slowly away from the cattle guard and back through the main gate to the middle of the ranch yard, the horse endeavoring awkwardly to figure out how to walk. Then, after a short discussion in low tones with a few of the other men, Roy handed the halter rope to someone else and went back to the bunkhouse to retrieve his pistol.

I just couldn't believe it when I saw Roy walking back to our silent group with his loaded gun. But I could believe it, too, and I offered no objection, because I knew there was no hope for a three-legged horse. And as one of the other hands held the halter rope short and tight, Roy took a position with a wide stance and squared the barrel of his pistol to the brow of the trembling animal. The horse looked right at him, and Roy shut his eyes. I can still picture how he squeezed them shut.

I knew when he opened them that he was pulling the trigger and a bullet was entering the horse's skull front and center, but all I saw was the horse begin to heave over backwards as I turned to flee. I heard it land on the dirt but I didn't see it because by then I was already running. I ran into the house and up to my room, afraid that this horrible ending to the evening's activities was my fault, and there I stayed until Pete and Mary got home later that night.

Mary and Pete weren't angry with me or with my brothers over the death of the horse. Another big crime that went unpunished. I think there was a lesson there, too, and I suppose at some level I learned it. Somewhere down inside my developing brain I believe I started to pick up on the fact that Mary and Pete were okay with us taking risks, and they were okay with us getting in over our heads, and they were probably even okay with really bad results, as long as we were giving it our all and doing it for the right reasons.

But that understanding was taking shape on a subconscious level, and I don't think I came away from the incident that night with any such insight. I was mystified at the time as to why I wasn't in big trouble when a horse had ended up dead with my help, and my horror over the maiming and shooting of the horse made me worry more, if anything, that I might make the wrong decisions about what did or did not need to be done on the ranch.

As for Roy, I suspected even when I was little that he was softhearted, and I was sorry about putting him through that particular chore. At the same time I wondered why he was the ranch hand, among several who were there that night, who took it on, given his temperament.

I admired all the ranch hands, quirky as some of them were, and felt like they were the boss of me—or at least, I'd have willingly done whatever they had asked me to do. I think most of them were reluctant to ask the boss's daughter to do anything, or maybe they didn't think I had much to offer even as free labor. As for myself, I didn't think I had any special status as the owners' granddaughter and daughter. I felt like I had almost no status when I was little because my responsibilities were relatively menial, usually along the lines of bringing garbage to the fire barrels and watching it burn.

Of course I went to school, and I actually made some effort there, but I found that other than home economics it was fairly easy, and I couldn't see how school work was making the world go around. Ranch work had such direct consequences compared to schoolwork, results that made themselves vividly known. The fields were irrigated and they grew; the cows were fed and they put on weight; the gate was left open and the horses got out.

The ranch hand who worked for our family the longest was Ray Mangum. In fact, he was employed by the owner of the Bar B C when my grandparents purchased it in the early 1950s, and he simply stayed on. So he was already a fixture on the property by the time my mother came back to the ranch with her husband in 1960.

Ray Mangum worked on the ranch from the time he was a teenager until the time he retired, and he lived there until the end of his life. According to Pete, "Ray never asked for anything," but my parents bought him a new pickup every three years or so, and Pete said he usually needed one by then. This was partly because he tended to drive the same speed regardless of any irregularities on the ground, and partly because, rather than turning his head to spit his tobacco juice out the window, he simply spat it on the floor of the truck. Over three or four years the residue would accumulate into a thick and putrid stain. Pete and Mary also eventually built a small house for Ray, which in his later years allowed him to move out of the bunkhouse and have some privacy and make his own coffee if he wanted to. As he aged Mary took care of him more like he was a family member than an employee.

He had no formal education beyond high school, but I often heard Mary and Pete marveling at the things Ray knew. He maintained a subscription to *National Geographic* magazine, and my parents said he read every issue, cover to cover, month after month, year after year. So he accumulated an amazing amount of knowledge on the most arcane subjects, and was probably better educated about the world beyond the borders of the ranch, the state, and indeed our continent than I suspect most of the teachers in the high school were.

When I heard Pete say to someone, not for the first time, that Ray Mangum read the *National Geographic* every month, I decided I was going to do the same thing. I went to our bookcases where we'd accumulated three or four dozen *National Geographic* magazines and leafed through them until I found a story about Prince Rainier marrying Grace Kelly in 1956. That was about the only story that interested me, and even then it was mostly because of the photos, and I didn't get much further.

Though Ray was well informed, he was not always talkative, and on certain subjects, such as his own discomfort, he was particularly mum. He and Pete and some other hands were moving cows in the snow one morning when Ray's horse fell down on the icy surface of the road, throwing Ray to the ground. Two or three hours later when they finished the job, Pete said it was time for lunch. But Ray said he'd be going into town and the hospital rather than to lunch, because he thought maybe his shoulder was broken. That diagnosis was subsequently confirmed with an X-ray, and he came back to the ranch in a sling.

But when I think of Ray, I don't think so much of winter but of summer, because I picture him mainly as our irrigator. I saw him riding out on horseback every morning and afternoon in the early summer with his big spade shovel counterbalanced over his shoulder. Our ranch was veined with narrow but deep irrigation ditches, decades old and mostly hand-dug, and he was a wizard with them. He made his irrigation dams with thick, treated canvas stapled onto long pine poles, and he'd learned over the years exactly where he needed to place them, anchored at the bottom by river rocks, so the ditches would overflow their banks and flood the pastures in a relatively precise manner, section by section. With gravity itself at his beck and call Ray could make the water go where he wanted. He knew the difference between up and down in places where it was imperceptible to nearly everyone else.

When he came in from irrigating the fields at lunchtime he would tie the reins off on his saddle horn, dismount, and go into the bunkhouse to wash his hands without tying up his horse. Then he would emerge, his horse still standing in the vicinity, and walk the fifty paces down the boardwalk to the cookhouse. He took a little more time at lunch than the other hands because he often went back out to irrigate at night. After eating he always drew a pouch of sweet tobacco from his shirt pocket and packed some into his pipe for a quiet smoke at the plank table after the others had left, with the peaceful sound of dishes being washed in the background.

My brother Brad, who now lives with his own family on the Lower Ranch, took me into the cookhouse a few years ago and, without saying anything, pulled my hand under the wooden edge of the long table at the place where Ray had always sat at the end of the bench. I felt for myself what Brad wanted me to recognize: the several deep grooves that had been worn over the years where Ray had struck a thousand wooden matches. And when I touched them a clear picture came into my mind: Ray filling the bowl of his pipe with tobacco and tamping it down with the blunt end of half a finger. Ray had lost part of three fingers to ranch work by the time I knew him, but a slight disfigurement didn't fascinate me as it might have other kids. I knew enough people without all their fingers that I assumed I might lose one or two fingers myself by the time I reached adulthood.

When Ray was finished with his lunch and his smoke, he would amble out of the cookhouse to locate his horse, usually not too far from where he'd first gotten off. His horse waited for him not just when he was in the cookhouse, but wherever he was working in the field, patiently standing by as Ray fitted a dam into a ditch, or dug pieces of sod to build up a bank and divert the water elsewhere. Ray had several different horses during the many years I knew him, and they were willing and patient partners, which perhaps says more about Ray than it does about them. He had a pinto horse named Dime who would actually jump into the back of Ray's pickup on command.

"Get in the goddamn truck," Ray would tell him, and the horse would jump in with his saddle on. Ray drove him around that way without even a stock rack on the sides of the truck bed. The canny horse just kept his balance, leaning into the corners as they went up the road.

But I don't suppose it was always a picnic to be Ray's horse. As he lit his pipe one day while helping to cut calves in the lane, he accidentally let a lit match fall from his hands. The match went into the hole at the front of his saddle, and pretty soon smoke was coming up from the saddle's gullet and his horse was twitching and jumping.

"Goddamn, my horse is on fire," he said gruffly to those who stared. Fortunately it was not so much the horse that had caught fire but the saddle blanket, so it was easily extinguished and the work continued.

One afternoon when Ray was at lunch, my brothers and I saw that Ray's big pinto horse, Dime, was loose. He'd rubbed off his bridle and was wandering tranquilly in the yard, the central dirt area which was framed by the barn, the cookhouse, our house, and a couple of pastures. Still too small to know much about Ray, his horse, or how he did things, we decided that we would do him the favor of tying up his horse. Rather than seek out the bridle which Dime had evidently discarded while Ray was in the cookhouse, we grabbed hold of a heavy rope which Ray kept knotted onto his saddle horn and tied the horse to a fence post with that.

The horse cooperated well enough when the three of us maneuvered him over to the fence, pushing and prodding on his hindquarters and shoulders, and he waited without fidgeting as we tied him to a sturdy post by the thick rope. But the moment we stepped away, Dime did a neat, thrusting sideways step and snapped the rope in two pieces. He then lowered his head and snatched another mouthful of grass from the side of the driveway, ignoring us. It seemed that a horse didn't like to be tied up by his back, and we slunk away, wishing we'd looked for the bridle instead, hoping Ray would be able to find another piece of short, thick rope to tie his canvas to.

I don't know what Ray made of it when he came out of the cookhouse, or how my brothers felt, but I was filled with a lasting guilt over the broken rope. It was not just that we'd ruined something that Ray needed for his job, but that we'd done the deed anonymously, and left Ray to wonder what happened.

In his later years Ray irrigated more out of a pickup truck than from horseback. He grew attached to the dog we had at the time, a sweet German shorthaired pointer named Molly, and she, like Ray's horses, seemed inclined to do what he wanted without the benefit of anything you'd classify as training from his end. When Ray came in for lunch in those days, he simply left his truck door standing open where he parked, so that Molly could get into the truck while he was in the cookhouse. She would wait for him, sitting upright in his front seat, and she was there at the ready when it was time for Ray to go back out in the fields. She enjoyed accompanying him on his rounds. One afternoon, having emerged from the cookhouse, Ray saw that Molly wasn't waiting on the seat despite the fact that he'd left the door open for her, so he whistled.

Not one to shirk, the hound came running up from the bog in the horse corral and headed straight for Ray's pickup truck. She jumped up onto the bench seat in a bound, and before Ray even realized that she was all wet, started shaking herself vigorously, spattering the interior of the truck, and Ray, with muddy water. Ray was indignant. He cursed her mightily, and although I'm sure she wasn't offended by his liberal use of the term *goddamn*, she hunched low in the seat at the tone and tenor of his voice, and didn't even want to look out the windows on their way through the gate.

But Molly redeemed herself by a mile the next day, according to Ray. He related the story with relish to Pete that evening.

"That's a smart dog," he said. "Before she got in my truck this afternoon she stood there and shook herself just as hard as she could. She was bone-dry! But goddamn if she didn't give herself a real good shaking. Yep," he continued, "she'd have been a real good dog if somebody'd got hold of her when she was a pup."

Ray was well aware of the fact that Pete and Mary had picked Molly right out of her litter, and had owned her ever since. But Pete enjoyed repeating Ray's story about Molly, and I heard it several times when I was growing up. It was clear from the first time that Ray's remark about what a squandered opportunity Molly represented didn't bother my dad.

Pete had not hired Ray; he'd inherited him. Ray was quite a bit older than Pete, who respected that fact. Pete also respected the fact that Ray had been on the ranch longer than he had, no matter that one person was the owner and the other was the employee. So Pete wasn't going to take offense at Ray's gibes; besides, he figured Ray was probably correct. Molly was unusually smart and could have been trained to do almost anything if someone had wanted to take the trouble.

Ray often got along better with animals than with machinery. "Tore the hell out of them" is how Pete described Ray's working relationship with trucks, tractors, and buck rakes. We had all kinds of machinery on the ranch, most of it second- or thirdhand, some of it army surplus, a lot of it homemade, none of it perfect. But my father, like most ranchers, was as good an auto mechanic as he was a cowboy. He kept things running even though it meant he spent many nights, after having worked all day, on his back on a creeper under the belly of a broken-down machine.

One of the pieces of heavy equipment we had was a Caterpillar dozer. The deep metal treads on its tracks could dig into and mow over just about any kind of obstacle or ground, so it was useful, but it also had the potential to be highly destructive, and Pete discouraged Ray from driving it to the point where Pete often made sure the key wasn't in the ignition.

But one spring Ray decided to dig himself a new ditch at the south end of our ranch, in a spot that was pretty low and somewhat boggy. Although it probably didn't need much in the way of man-made irrigation, it could perhaps have benefited from having the water gathered up. The keys were in the Cat that day, and Ray hooked up the ditcher to the back end of the machine and started the five-mile-an-hour trek down through the fields.

Dragging a ditcher is almost like dragging a big V-shaped plow, but it has wheels on levers so you can raise and lower it, which allows you to tow it without digging in. In fact, it's important that you do raise it if it starts to dig in too deeply because the ditcher can get you slowed down to the point where your own power works against you, and pretty soon, rather than digging a ditch behind you, you're digging a hole underneath you with the tracks of your own Cat. Ray didn't ever believe he'd gotten to a point where he needed to raise the ditcher, however; that day he just kept at the throttle even when the tracks started turning in place. Eventually he had the Cat buried above its tracks, a feat you wouldn't think possible if you stood in a machinery yard and looked for a while at the way a Cat is designed and constructed. It probably can't be done without a ditcher.

Ray dug himself in with the help of the ditcher that day until the Cat finally high-centered itself on the frame, although, as my father reported when he surveyed the scene later that day, even the frame was partially buried thanks to the boggy ground. It was perplexing for him to have been driving up the road, Pete remembers, and to look out across the field to notice only the top two-thirds of a big diesel Caterpillar emerging, it seemed, from under the willow bottoms.

Getting the Cat out of that southern corner, which we called the Vogel field after the family that homesteaded it, took a day's work. Pete managed to hoist the front end of the Cat up a little with the leverage of its own hydraulic dozer, and when he had just enough space, he had the other hands throw a big log down under the front end of the tracks. He'd hauled a truckload of logs down there, and one by one he had the hired men who were helping him throw them under the Cat as he inched it forward and gave them another six inches of room at a time. By this method he eventually managed to drive it completely up on top of the logs and out of its hole.

About a year later my father, mother, and several ranch hands were sitting in the cookhouse at supper time. Ray was there in his spot at the end of the table, and people started telling stories about one another in the relaxed atmosphere of full stomachs and the day's work over with. After listening to the others for a while Ray took his pipe out of his mouth and cleared his throat, getting everyone's attention.

"I just remember when Pete got that goddamn Cat stuck down in the Vogel field," he said, and resumed smoking.

For years my father enjoyed telling that story—how Ray had blamed him for nearly burying the Cat—and I laughed along with everyone else, but I wasn't sure I understood why it didn't bother my father. In fact, when I first heard it, I thought it was outlandish, given all the work that Pete had had to do to get the Cat out of the bog. I finally asked Pete, much later, why he wasn't upset about the way Ray revised history.

"I don't think he was revising it," Pete explained. "He was telling it the way he remembered it." Which Pete thought was not only funny, but understandable, given Ray's seniority.

6

Wrecks and Near-Wrecks

As FAR AS I KNEW NO RANCH HANDS WERE VERY SERIOUSLY HURT IN OUR employ, beyond broken bones. Marty, of Marty and Wayne, did fall off the top of a twenty-ton haystack in a high wind and break his back, and as I've said, slight maimings such as lost fingers weren't uncommon, but other than that we carried on in what some people might've thought of as a dangerous environment. I didn't think about it as being dangerous at the time; I just knew that Brad and Matt and I had better watch out for ourselves.

We did watch out, but accidents happened nonetheless. Brad had his forehead opened up to the skull when he was just a baby, falling off the back of a horse where he was riding tandem with my father, and under the galloping hooves. I was knocked out cold when I slipped off the top of the hay wagon as a toddler and landed headfirst on the frozen driveway.

Matt, though, got hurt the worst of us three.

I couldn't think of exactly how old Matt was when he had his big tractor wreck, and since he's rather busy as governor, I hate to bother him about trivial things, so I asked Pete.

"Well, I know he'd been driving the tractor in the hayfield all day," Pete said, "so he must've been thirteen or fourteen."

"No," I said, "because that would've made me fifteen or sixteen, and I know for sure I was a lot younger than that."

Pete paused. "So you're saying Matt was what? Eleven?" His tone conveyed the unlikely nature of that, of an eleven-year old working all day in the hayfield.

I had to agree with Pete on that, and I didn't really trust my own memory. So I finally called Matt and asked him how old he was when he nearly killed himself on the tractor, and he reported that he was nine.

He had indeed been driving an old John Deere tractor in the hayfield all day and when he finally got off work wanted to do something for fun. So he decided to drive the tractor up East Gros Ventre Butte to pick raspberries. There was a wild raspberry patch high on the butte, which during a two-week span of August, right in the middle of haying season, was overflowing with heavy red berries. The plants were so hardy that when Teton County asked if they could quarry rock from the area to shore up the levee on the Gros Ventre River, five miles north of our house, my parents said yes. It wasn't long before raspberries were proliferating along the riverbanks where they'd dumped the rock. I was a big walker so I always walked if I wanted to go to the raspberry patch, but Brad and Matt would take a piece of equipment if it was available.

Matt was driving down the twisty road from the raspberry patch when he realized he'd picked up too much momentum. Though he was only nine years old he was a good driver, and he knew better than to completely rely on the old brakes of the John Deere, so he took it out of third gear to downshift. But with the clutch depressed for just a moment, he picked up even more speed, and he couldn't wrench the gear shift into second, or even back into third.

So he hurtled along, driving for all he was worth on the very narrow and crude dirt road that in some places was nothing but switchbacks. His tractor was in neutral and the brake, though he stomped on it, was doing almost nothing to slow him down. Finally, at a hard turn to the right, his tractor went to the left, off the steep embankment, and down the hill into some huge boulders. Matt was thrown over the front end of the tractor and luckily for him landed in a big willow bush, which apparently saved his life. The tractor when it came to a stop was upside down.

I didn't think that this was too big a deal until all kinds of people started calling the house over the next few days, some of them from other towns, asking how Matt was doing. I'm afraid until the calls started coming in I was not overcome with worry. *Oh, Matt's wrecked his tractor,* I thought.

They'll patch him up, but it sounds like the tractor's a total loss. Even though it had slowed him way down when his tractor met up with the willow, Matt kept going and hit the rocks. He was hurt pretty badly and spent the better part of a week in the hospital with head and other injuries.

I feel lucky I didn't get killed in one particular tractor mishap myself, even though unlike Matt, I was on flat ground, not even moving. When I was first learning to pull a side-delivery rake in the hayfield I started off in fourth gear one time, thinking I was in second, and then compounded that mistake by accidentally popping the clutch as I pushed the throttle up. The whole front end of the tractor came right off the ground and might've gone all the way over backwards if I hadn't had the big rake with its rigid tongue hooked on behind. I was lucky—luckier than Matt.

There were certain things I really did fear and stayed away from. The acetylene welding torch, the culvert that sucked the creek under Spring Gulch Road, the sticks of dynamite I sometimes saw lined up in boxes on the workbench in the shop.

Dynamite was Ray Mangum's department, probably his favorite one, though he didn't always use it as cautiously as my father recommended.

Ray blew up the bunkhouse septic tank with four sticks of dynamite one day, although Pete had explicitly told him not to use dynamite to clear out the clogged tank. This was in the days when telephones were still tethered to the wall, and while my father and Ray were trying to carefully dig around the backed-up tank with the backhoe, Mary came out to announce that Pete had an important phone call which required his going back to the house.

Before he left the scene, my father reiterated to Ray that it would be a bad idea to try and clear out the septic tank with dynamite, and he went to take his call. It was when he was in the middle of his telephone conversation over at the house that he heard the explosion. He wasn't halfway back over to the bunkhouse, having abruptly excused himself from the phone, before he could smell the full extent of the damage. The septic tank was more than cleared out. It was obliterated.

For Ray, though, dynamite was a helpful tool that did the job quicker than most other tools, and he was creative about the uses he put it to. He even dug post holes for fences with dynamite, and my brother Brad at the age of ten was sent along to help him. Brad described how Ray would use a sledgehammer to drive a steel rod into the ground where he wanted the fence post. He'd then remove the rod and drop in a quarter stick of lit dynamite and quickly cover the top with a rock. The rock, reportedly, contained the explosion just enough to dig a fine post hole, even though the rock itself flew high into the air. This only worked if the ground was pretty hard, but I suppose if the ground was soft Ray would've used a post-hole digger like everyone else.

Ray got the idea at one point that a person could also dig ditches with dynamite, faster than with the ditcher. Pete put the kibosh on that one. But other demolition did need to be done from time to time, and fortunately for Ray and his particular temperament, dynamite was usually at hand on our place, and on other cattle ranches that I knew of. Ray used dynamite to blow up beaver dams in certain instances, because the beavers, enterprising and willful, often did not want to build their dams where Ray wanted them. And he wasn't sorry if he saw a beaver itself flung up in the air, turning end over end in the maelstrom of an exploding dam.

Dynamite was also used to blow up cattle on the rare occasion that they died out on the range, so their carcasses wouldn't be a magnet for scavengers, in particular, bears. Our summer cattle range was not on our property; it was on public land, and some of it was in Grand Teton National Park. The Park Service didn't want bears getting accustomed to the taste of beef, but that was out of concern for the bears, not the cattle. Bears that were used to being fed became a dangerous nuisance and had to be airlifted out of the park and relocated, or even destroyed.

So they called us pretty quickly when they came across one of our cows that had died within park boundaries, and if the animal was in an area considered too environmentally sensitive for us to even drive one of our vehicles over to pick up the carcass, they wanted us to go out on foot with dynamite and literally blow the animal to smithereens. A complete erasure of the cow, even though it required a sizable explosion in a sometimes-pristine area, was necessary in order to protect the bears, the natural inhabitants, from the consequences of their interaction with cattle, the interlopers.

One day, as an adult, Brad took some dynamite in his pickup to Grand Teton National Park where one of our cows had died. He had forgotten his wallet, and, having no way to pay the park entrance fee, explained to the ranger that although he had no money, he was there at the behest of the Park Service itself.

"They called me to come and blow up a cow," he said.

The earnest park ranger looked blankly at Brad through the little window of the government hut. She didn't believe that this could actually be his mission—that what he'd just described could really be something he'd been summoned by her bosses to do.

"Look in the back of my truck," he said. "I've got fifty pounds of dynamite." Oddly enough, that did it for her.

"Go ahead," she said authoritatively, waving her hand.

I never had to blow up a cow myself, but I felt that I'd inherited a pyromaniac gene which might've been passed down from my grandfather. Granddad didn't like to have too much junk around, and he always liked to light bonfires to get rid of it when there was finally a big enough pile of stuff that, even in Granddad's estimation, could not be reused. Without any garbage pickup at the time, burning was the only option for getting rid of trash, besides burying it or stockpiling it, and most ranchers did a little of all three. But for Granddad, burning it was ideal. We probably have my grandmother to thank for the fact that the whole ranch never went up in flames.

Grammy had a deep fear of the buildings catching fire, and thanks to her influence Granddad was more cautious than his own nature would have otherwise dictated. Even on a day that promised rain, Grammy might kneel down to rub the grass between her fingers. The words "Pretty dry, Cliff," from my grandmother would usually warn him off of having a bonfire.

But finally the day, or even better, the night, would come when he'd light them. We'd walk up the draw to where the dump was, across the road from my grandparents' house, just above the site of our doomed underground fort. In this particular dump we collected mostly old wood such as logs and boards that were so splintered, or short, or simply old, that we couldn't make a use for them anymore. Someone would bring along a small can of gasoline from our gas pump, and matches.

I felt like a barbarian when the fire caught on to the huge pile of lumber and other debris and shot into the night sky. I probably have some arsonist in me, but I believe there's nothing like the visceral thrill of a fire with flames leaping to fifty feet when you've set it yourself. Even the adults seemed mesmerized by the spectacle. I was not as cautious as my grandmother and had little fear of fire. My brothers and I built fires on a pretty regular basis—partly because we liked to go camping up in the draw on West Gros Ventre Butte, and building and tending a fire was the essential activity of camping. We would typically cook dinner by opening a can of beans and then, with leather gloves on, placing it right in the flames.

I often carried matches around with me whether I was camping or not, because we incinerated all the household garbage in a pair of old oil drums, and I was usually the one on trash duty. I didn't really like hauling garbage in paper grocery sacks which were often soggy on the bottom, but I enjoyed putting fire to the whole thing once I had it in the barrel. First, just a bit of smoke, and then some crackling flames, and finally a low roar as the heat swirled in the drum, fueled like a blast furnace by oxygen sucked in through the rusted-out holes near the bottom. I enjoyed it a little too much, I guess, but ultimately I did learn to be choosier about the things I set on fire.

I remember one time when someone filling the tank of their pickup at the gas pump had let it overflow, and had left a large puddle of gas on the ground adjacent to the pump. It was shallow but about five feet wide. I'm sure whoever had left the puddle of fuel realized it would eventually evaporate in the summer sun, but when Matt and Brad and I came upon it, we stood around discussing what should be done. One of them suggested we could get rid of the gas puddle pretty quickly by tossing a match in, and that was all it took for me. A half-second later we had flames higher than ourselves, a blazing inferno that surprised even Brad and Matt from what I could tell, because they jumped away. As for me, it was then that I realized three feet away from the gas pump was not a good place to have started a blazing inferno.

The vet was next door at the barn looking after one of our horses, and he had water tanks mounted on the back of his truck, along with a sprayer hose. He saw the wall of flames and reacted immediately, so the fire was put out just about the time my mother came running over from the house. She'd been making lunch when she'd looked out the kitchen window to see a plume of black smoke rising over the trees.

After that, everyone wanted to know who'd thrown the match in; who, if they were at all sane, would have started a big fire next to the gas pump? When I say that my mother was reluctant to tell me how to do things, I don't mean she was reluctant to convey her disappointment when I did something stupid. She didn't go on and on about it, though. The words "You what?" were sufficient to let me know her opinion. And there was no punishment that day at the gas pump—just the identification of the idiot.

I realized after the fact that my brothers, too, thought it was dim-witted of me to have gone ahead and done what they had merely verbalized. I was more regretful of that—of not having known the difference—than I was about having started the fire. As soon as the idea of burning the gas puddle had been mentioned, I'd seized what I thought was the glory of torching it before anyone else could, so I could hardly have mentioned to the vet or to Mary that it had been Matt and Brad's idea, nor did I feel that they should share in the blame (although I think this was one of the few times I felt that way).

I saw more than once that accidental fires had the same destructive potential as the ones you set on purpose. Our calving barn at the Double T burned down one morning after a freshly branded and disoriented calf bolted from the branding chute. The calf ran over the propane heater for the branding irons, knocking it over and disconnecting the hose, which then spewed lit fuel erratically onto the side of the barn like a blowtorch, and the building went up like paper.

Less spectacularly, our haystacks sometimes burned up. At that time they were just twenty-ton piles of loose hay with a fence around the bottom, and if the hay hadn't been dried thoroughly enough before being stacked, it could begin to decompose in the middle, a heat-generating process which sometimes caused the entire stack to actually combust

Gathering cows at the south end of the Bar B C. HANSEN FAMILY COLLECTION.

P.C. Hansen on his favorite buckskin in the early 1930s. JACKSON HOLE HISTORICAL SOCIETY.

Clifford Helen   Sylvia   Robert   Peter   Ordene

P.C. and Sylvia with family; Granddad is in back row at left. HANSEN FAMILY COLLECTION.

Sylvia, with Granddad as a boy, doing dishes after the trail riders have moved off with the cattle (c. 1920). JACKSON HOLE HISTORICAL SOCIETY (FROM EDITH STINNETT COLLECTION).

Hired hands and Hansen family members at cow camp; Sylvia is on horseback, furthest left; P.C. is on foot, middle photo. HANSEN FAMILY COLLECTION.

P.C. and Sylvia with some of their children and grandchildren in 1935. Grand-dad, holding baby Mary, is at left. HANSEN FAMILY COLLECTION.

Grammy soon after marrying Granddad and coming to the ranch. HANSEN FAMILY COLLECTION.

Wintertime feeding at the Bar B C. Granddad takes a turn driving the team while a hand pitches hay. HANSEN FAMILY COLLECTION.

Grammy and Granddad at a governors' conference in the early 1960s. HANSEN FAMILY COLLECTION.

Granddad's photo, taken for a news story after he was elected governor in 1962. HANSEN FAMILY COLLECTION.

Grammy and Granddad as newlyweds at cow camp. A tradition involved placing charcoal from the campfire on the bride's nose. HANSEN FAMILY COLLECTION.

Pete was the "Camel Man" in the early 1960s. MEAD FAMILY COLLECTION.

Photo of Mary taken for the cover of *Farm Journal* magazine in the mid-1960s. FARM JOURNAL MAGAZINE.

Mary working her horse Pardner in the corral. MEAD FAMILY COLLECTION.

Mary and Pete at the horse barn, early 1960s. MEAD FAMILY COLLECTION.

Pete and Mary's wedding in Jackson in 1958. MEAD FAMILY COLLECTION.

Muffy as a baby, being passed around after lunch on the cattle drive. From left to right: Leona Williams (Muffy's godmother), Pete, Phyllis (Mrs. Brownie) Brown, Grammy. BROWN FAMILY COLLECTION.

Muffy, Brad, and Matt milking Posy (c. 1970). JACKSON HOLE NEWS & GUIDE.

Muffy at age thirteen, with her yearling colt, Dusty; Brad and Matt also had new colts. MEAD FAMILY COLLECTION.

Brad driving one of the ancient Farmall tractors. JACKSON HOLE NEWS & GUIDE.

Pete, Brad, and Matt (at left), moving the herd up through Mormon Row with other cowboys. HANSEN FAMILY COLLECTION.

Granddad and Roy Martin in 1988. HANSEN FAMILY COLLECTION.

View of Lower Ranch buildings and fields; Grammy and Granddad's "new" house is at bottom, surrounded by trees. MEAD FAMILY COLLECTION.

Belle pole-bending in the Driggs, Idaho, rodeo in 2010, at age twelve. PETER MEAD.

Joe steer-riding in the Island Park, Idaho, rodeo in 2010, at age ten. PETER MEAD.

The Pig Farm on the wrong side of the Tetons, with pig barn at left, horse barn at right. MICHAEL FERRO.

The M Lazy M buckle that Pete had made for Mary. BELLE FERRO

from the inside out. Sometimes you could save some of the hay by tearing the stack apart but usually that was too risky; a sudden influx of oxygen to the smoldering core could bring about the exact wrong result. So typically my parents just let them smolder, and they could smolder for weeks. You could smell the slow burn up at the golf course five miles away, if the wind happened to be blowing in the right direction, and someone said it was like God smoking a cigar.

It seeped into my consciousness, in increments of blown-up septic tanks and burned haystacks, that things on the ranch did go wrong without my help, both because of accidents, and also because people besides myself were capable of making mistakes. Even Ray Mangum, and even my mother.

When we drove snowmobiles up to the Bar Double R in the winter Mary was often in the lead, partly because it was hard to keep up with her. One winter she was pulling a sled behind her snowmobile, packed with all the supplies necessary to see us through our stay at the snowed-in ranch. She was driving so fast over the rough terrain of the Gros Ventre that she didn't even realize it when the sled came unhitched and turned over, dumping all our food, clothing, and other supplies into the snow.

Brad came upon the debris field first, and just about had the sled repacked when my mother came roaring back, having finally realized somewhere up the road that her load had been lightened. They got her sled hitched up again and off she went, but without driving any differently, and when Brad came upon the supplies scattered across the road a second time—with Mary nowhere in sight—he was really mad at her.

I enjoyed the fact that my mother on the very rare occasion messed up, but I noticed that messing up didn't slow her down. Success in my parents' world seemed to be more about sticking with it, about going at it full throttle, than what you did wrong or right on any given day. Becoming aware of that made it a bit easier as I grew to find my place.

What also made it easier to find my place was the fact that there were other people besides my parents who set the example, who helped me along—people who befriended me, and in some cases helped raise me. Most memorably there were the Martins.

7

The Martins

THE MARTINS WERE OUR CLOSEST NEIGHBORS. SINCE THEY WORKED FOR us, they lived on our property, but their house was a mile up the road at the place some people called the Double T, but I called the Martins'. They had two older children who had left home by the time I was old enough to have playmates, but their two youngest boys were around most of the years that I was.

The only other neighbors we had along the several miles of Spring Gulch Road were the Lucases, who had property in between the Lower Ranch and the Bar B C. Rod Lucas owned land on the west side of the road, and his brother Phil, on the east. Rod's wife Joyce was a benevolent presence on Spring Gulch, and I knew her better than her sister Betty, who lived on the other side of the road, having married Rod's brother Phil. Joyce's house was approximately three miles up the road from ours, which was about my limit on a one-speed bicycle, so I used Joyce and Rod's ranch as my turnaround and refreshment point. Betty and Phil's house, at nearly five miles away, was a little outside my range.

I figured the Rod Lucas family was quite a bit better off than we were, mainly on the grounds that their barn was painted red. Our barns were not painted and the wood logs and planks showed all the signs of having been at the weather's mercy for however many decades they'd been standing there. It was just further evidence of how old everything was at our place and, as I've said, a prolonged existence was not something I valued at the time. The Lucases' barn, being red, seemed as good as new.

Where the Martins lived was even closer than bicycle distance, though, if you liked walking, and I did. I walked to their house more often than I biked to it, and in the summertime I could shorten the one-mile distance somewhat by cutting up through the field. It was, as I'd learned, "up" to get to their house. But the rise in altitude was not perceptible, and I knew where the ditch crossings were, and I enjoyed the journey. I spent more time at the Martins' than at either of the Lucases'.

The Martin family patriarch, Roy Martin, was a cowboy, but I have to elaborate on what that terminology means in this instance, because I remember the discussions that sometimes took place at our dinner table. It wasn't just that we disdained drugstore cowboys, of which Jackson always had its share. On top of that, every once in a while Mary and Pete hired an employee who might've been a good rider but who turned out to be mostly interested in chasing cows around on horseback. Not only did this not begin to cover what ranching was all about, it wasn't even what being a cowboy was all about. In Pete and Mary's estimation, you couldn't be much of a cowboy if you had plenty of respect for horses but mostly disdain for cows. You had to have an understanding of cattle, some empathy, too, and ideally, some medical knowledge.

A good cowboy was able to get cattle to go where he wanted as unobtrusively as possible, preferably without scaring them. The first thing Mary and Pete taught me to do when we were herding cattle was to observe where they were headed by their own volition. If they were already going the right way, there was no reason to start whooping and hollering and running up on them with your horse. If the cows needed to be turned through a gate or didn't want to cross the creek, then yes, you made your presence known.

It's not like my education in herding cattle involved any preliminary classwork before going out into the field, or any practice before finding myself in the middle of an actual cattle drive where lives were at stake, or anything much at all in the way of actual narrative. For the most part Pete and Mary taught by example—meaning you'd be hopelessly lost if you didn't pay close attention. But for the rest of it they used essentially the same method they used with the cows. You didn't really hear much from them unless you did something wrong, and at that point they made their presence known.

My parents—and my mother in particular—were gentler and quieter with their cows than what I saw on other ranches. Pete and Mary didn't own cow dogs, and they didn't like to have our cows on the run because of dogs or anything else. Maybe that's not what some of the younger ranch hands expected, but if they didn't learn that way of tending to cattle they didn't last with Pete and Mary. Roy Martin lasted for six decades.

I always thought Roy looked more at home on the back of a horse than on his own two feet. He rode in a completely relaxed posture, like he'd been sitting there for days. His face had a friendly look, and he had gentlemanly manners even though his stubbly chin was often stained with the dribblings of a chew. I never saw him out of cowboy boots, and he was only out of a hat at the dinner table. He seemed to be altogether unexcitable, quiet in his speech and deliberate in his movements. I always felt comfortable around him.

Mrs. Martin's name was Zelda. For a long time she was the only person I'd ever seen with red hair, and when I was little this had the illogical effect of frightening me, but I think that was also because she often seemed to be hollering in her high-pitched voice at her son, Will, two years older than I was. Later in life I noticed that the hair coming just out of her scalp was not the vivid color I'd always known, but white, and probably had been for some time, and that softened my perceptions. Moreover, now that I'm a parent I can imagine that Will, who was referred to by a number of people as Wild Will, often needed hollering at. In any case, my own mother never had any sympathy for me when I told her how Mrs. Martin hollered at us; without even hearing Zelda's side of the story she acted like she was solidly on the side of Zelda.

The person I was most fond of in their family was Will's older brother, Roy Reed. Reed was his middle name, but everyone used both in order to avoid confusing him with his father. The main thing about Roy Reed was that, although he could ride any horse, he didn't seem to have the cowboy aspirations that were typical of the rest of us. He didn't ever seem to think of himself or to present himself as a cowboy, despite his surroundings, his bloodline, and the expectations of everyone he knew. He thought of himself as an Indian.

His fascination with Indians (at the time we hadn't yet heard the more correct term, Native Americans) must have started when he was pretty little, and it never left him. Even though he rode his horse with a Western saddle, he often covered that up with a striped blanket, and he sometimes had a variety of authentic-looking Plains Indian accoutrements such as feathers tied into his horse's mane, and beaded medallions to dress up his bridle. Sometimes his horse itself would be decorated with paint in the Indian way, with circles around the eyes and handprints on its sides. And Roy Reed made costumes for himself and for us by the armload. He educated himself as to all the Indian designs and their meanings and taught himself to do beautiful beadwork. He didn't often have buckskin to work with, but in its place he used a wheat-colored canvas salvaged from our worn-out irrigation dams, and the effect was convincing.

Not that all of Roy Reed's Indian projects were merely decorative; he also made tepees and weapons. He became fairly proficient at making bows and arrows, and got to where he could shoot his arrows a good distance and still rely on their trajectory. He made many sets of arrows and some truly wicked-looking spears, though I never saw him try to harm a living thing; he was too kindhearted.

I did see him harm a living thing one time, but that was an accident which no one could have foreseen. A group of us—Roy Reed, Will, their girl cousin Terry, and Brad and Matt and I—had hiked about halfway up the steep and thickly wooded hillside across the road from the Double T. Most of us needed to get our breath at that point, but restless Will decided to see if he could scrabble up one of the many aspen trees that surrounded us. This was not an easy undertaking, as aspens growing in bunches tend to have puny branches that break off easily, even if the trunk has gotten pretty big around, leaving you nothing but a jagged stub for a hand- or foothold.

With the noise of Will's assault upon the aspen tree going on in the background, my brothers stood by, hoping for a turn with Roy Reed's bow and arrow, and I was distracted with adjusting my wig. As a practical matter Mary usually made me keep my hair short when I was little, but Roy Reed knew that I yearned for long hair and had made me a black wig out of hair that someone had pulled from the tail of a bay horse. The hair had been left in a burlap bag in one of the equipment sheds at the Double T, which is where Roy Reed found it. Horsehair had been saved for stuffing cushions at one time and there must've been somebody around who was still in the habit. Roy Reed gathered, combed, and shaped a bunch of those rough black strands and tied them into a ponytail so it would stay on my head. I didn't care that it was stringy and unclean—what I liked was that it was long.

Mary herself was way too pragmatic to have any use for long hair, and I suppose she might've had at least some distaste for the idea of a dirty cap of horsehair going around on her daughter's head all summer. But despite all that she didn't stop me from wearing Roy Reed's wig, and I was quite devoted to it at the time.

Roy Reed decided to see how far he could shoot an arrow, but since we were in a stand of trees and on a hill, he shot it straight up into the sky rather than over ground. I held onto my wig and put my head back to watch it streak up like a rocket until I lost sight of it.

Just then Will came down out of the tree.

"Whatcha doin'?" he asked, not picking up anything in particular from the fact that our five faces were all turned skyward. We lowered our gazes to Will then, but before a response to his question could be uttered, the arrow came down with a *thunk* onto Will's head and stopped, sticking upright in the top of his skull.

It turned out not to have been too deeply sunk into his skull, because his older and taller cousin Terry was able to yank it out in one try. It was only at the point when blood started pouring over his face that Will decided he was not happy. Terry grabbed him by the hand and dragged him down the hillside, screaming and crying, though I wasn't sure, standing there as mute as a fence post, if the cries were coming from Will or from Terry.

Will's family wasn't one to make a big commotion over scalp wounds, but the arrowhead had gone a bit beyond that. So his mother did take him to the doctor and found he was a good eighth of an inch from serious trouble. I know Roy Reed felt bad about the whole thing, but I think some of the rest of us had to begin stifling our laughter before Terry had Will as far as the road.

"I guess he'll learn to look up next time," I said later to Roy Reed, not thinking what a bad idea that would have been.

Roy Reed, perhaps because he was the oldest in the group, or because he had the most interesting outlook, quite often took the lead when we were little, and that resulted in some activities which I don't believe we could have dreamed up on our own. One summer we had an old Hereford bull die in the pasture next to the shop, apparently from testicular cancer. He'd been sick for a while, and although the vet had done what he could, the adults agreed the bull was a goner. He'd been sequestered in this odd pasture away from the other stock.

After the bull finally died, but before my father had a chance to haul him off to the bone pile, Roy Reed started explaining to Brad and Matt and me the Indian method of skinning an animal, and with that, the fate of the bull's carcass was determined.

According to Roy Reed, the Indians could just about get the hide off a buffalo with one big, steady pull after they'd made cuts around the neck and all four legs, and then connected them with a cut down the belly. That seemed amazing, but then again quite plausible to us as junior highers, and we were able to convince my father that the removal of the beast to the bone pile had to wait.

The bull had been dead a little while before we got around to skinning him the Indian way, and he must have smelled, but that wouldn't have been any impediment. A lot of things smelled on the ranch, and most people didn't react, even though many of the smells were quite strong. Diesel fuel, cut hay, the calving barn. All of these things had their smell, and it wasn't so much that they were good or bad, it was that they were objective evidence of something specific. I knew it if my dad had had to shoot an animal because I could smell the gunpowder and the blood. My mother didn't have to tell me if she'd been branding, haying, or frying chicken.

The smell of dead things was particularly common, I think, because a lot of animals such as ranch cats liked to crawl under a shed or the barn floor before they expired, installing their carcasses and the accompanying smell as a reminder, not removable, of their having lived, and died. One summer over by the bunkhouse there was the smell of a dead animal for the longest time, but if you moved away from the bunkhouse it actually got stronger. That was strange—the opposite of what we were used to—and no one could figure out where it was coming from. Finally one of the ranch hands looked up and saw that a poor cat had been electrocuted twenty feet up on the light pole, which stood about ten feet away from the bunkhouse, and remarkably, there it had stayed.

But the other reason the smell of death was so common was due to the fondness our dogs had for it. If any kind of an animal had died, whether one of our own or something in the wild, our dogs found it. The odor of death was a siren's call to nearly every dog we ever owned, and they couldn't resist wiggling their backs in whatever dead thing they could find, large or small, domestic or wild, soaking up that smell and bringing it home for all the rest of us to take notice of. I've gathered since then that it's not known exactly why dogs do this, but for us, the dogs served as messengers. Something has died, they told us.

So without being bothered too much by the smell of decomposition, I'm sure, Brad and Roy Reed took Roy Reed's Buck knife and made the prescribed cuts in the bull's thick hide while Matt and I watched. That was supposed to have been about all there was to it; the hide would just come right off like an orange peel, we thought. Yet it did not, and after everyone had gotten a turn yanking their hardest on the nape of the bull's neck at the leading edge of what was to be our new tepee rug, we determined that none of us was physically as strong as the Indians and went to fetch some machinery.

As I've described, we pretty much had the run of the old shop, along with all the scrap metal, scrap wood, screws, nails, soldering iron, welding torch, jigsaw, grinder, and drill press. We knew better, but it was easy to operate as if everything there had been assembled for our own personal use in order that we could make forts, build rafts, or skin animals.

Whatever our pressing needs might be. Other than my lack of a relationship with the welding torch we were pretty proficient with the tools, and we had free access to the stash of scrap wood and metal.

We decided that if we got a good rope knotted onto the nape of the bull's neck, we could probably get the hide pulled off by tying the rope around the ball hitch on the back of Mary's four-wheel-drive Jeep Wagoneer. We weren't strong enough to hold the bull in place while the four-wheel-drive pulled in the other direction, so my brother rummaged around in the shop until he found something that would solve that problem—in this case, a sharp iron stake that was a foot long. What use a stake of this size might have normally had on the ranch I don't know, but it seemed, like so many other items we could find on any given day in the wondrous inventory of the old shop, tailor-made for the objective we had in mind.

We brought the stake, along with a sledgehammer, back to the site of our operation and it fell to Roy Reed, the strongest and frankly the bravest, to hammer the stake through the bull's nose at the nostrils and into the ground of the pasture.

When he finished the job it looked to me like that bull's nose wasn't ever going anywhere, no matter what forces of nature or man might be brought to bear. But then, to our consternation, it did. Every time Roy Reed put the Wagoneer in gear and started to pull on the rope, a little bit of the hide would peel from the muscle, but a little bit of the nose-stake would also issue from the ground. We couldn't make enough progress on the hide before the stake was pulled completely out of the ground, even though Matt and I each tried more than once to put all our skinny weight on it and anchor it down.

So we went to fetch another item of machinery. In retrospect, the backhoe seems like overkill, but perhaps it was the first vehicle Brad came to in the shop yard.

There was another fifteen minutes of fuss with ropes, chains, and equipment before we began round two with the stubborn animal. The rope we'd tied onto his hide was still hooked to the Wagoneer, but in addition to that, a heavy chain was hooked around the iron stake and looped around the bucket of the backhoe. The bull was attached to two pieces of machinery, each of them poised to go in different directions. It would have made for an elaborate implement of torture had we been medieval dungeon keepers, but we were simply trying to do what the Indians had done. At the time I'm sure I didn't ask myself how the Indians managed to do everything without the use of Jeeps and backhoes, and I didn't ask myself if a sharp knife, such as the one I had in my own pocket, might've come in handy.

The plan was for Roy Reed to slowly drive the Wagoneer in one direction while Brad operated the hydraulic controls that pulled the backhoe bucket in the other direction, keeping the tension on the nose-stake and its chain taut the whole time. The bull would finally be made to stay put, and the hide would have no choice but to peel off.

Matt and I stood by to watch. My eyes were focused on the white fibrous matter that seemed to be fixing the bull's thick hide to its muscle, waiting to see further signs of progress given what must surely be the foolproof method we had now employed.

Both machines were engaged. I was watching the hide stretch and finally start to pull away from all that tough connective tissue, when suddenly there was a wet ripping and snapping sound. Although my gaze had been stuck fast to our long-awaited progress with the hide, I couldn't help but notice that the bull's head was gone. I turned and saw it at that moment, overhead and to my left, up in the air. It was stunning to look at, a dripping head with horns swinging wildly to and fro, by its nose, at the end of the chain we'd tied to the backhoe bucket.

We'd had enough then, not so much because we were put off by the unplanned beheading, but because the entire project had lost, literally, its moorings. We never did discuss the idea of simply taking a knife and skinning the animal properly because we weren't nearly as motivated by the prospect of ending up with the hide as we were by doing something the Indian way.

Brad and Roy Reed put the heavy equipment away, along with the chain, the rope, and the stake. We left the bull's head next to his body so Pete wouldn't miss it, although I don't know that anyone ever offered him an explanation for what he'd find there.

I'm sure a lot of children would get in trouble for that sort of thing (yes, I realize not many children ever do that sort of thing), but by then I knew we wouldn't. It was like the giant mess we'd left for my father in the draw, when the bull had fallen through the lumber roof of our underground fort. As long as we put a good-size portion of our own blood, sweat, and tears into something, even if it went horribly wrong, we were probably in the clear. What might be more remarkable than not getting in trouble for it, though, is how little we discussed it with Mary and Pete. I don't recollect ever discussing this incident with them, in fact. I didn't run over to the house to tell Mary that we'd just taken the head off a bull, nor did it come up as a topic at the supper table that evening. Despite the fact that Pete had to clean up after us, it was, for the most part, our own business.

The decapitation of the bull brings to mind the fact that with most of our escapades, including this one, there were no other girls involved. As far as I recall, it was not any hardship growing up as the only girl among my brothers and the two Martin boys, although it didn't exactly put me in a leadership position.

It would make sense to say that Mary was my role model, but she wasn't—at least, not in a practical sense. That would have been like saying Willa Cather or Emily Dickinson was my role model; these are people you might admire, but you don't really hope to emulate them. It's more like you run along after them, trying to get close enough to understand how it is they're doing what they're doing. Mary seemed to not only know everything that needed to be done on the ranch, and how to do it, but also to think those things were at all times completely self-evident, whereas I expected I'd have to figure everything out by trial and error, one thing at a time.

If anything, my brother Brad was my role model, because I continued to think that if Brad could figure things out, then surely I, only one year younger, had some hope of figuring them out too. My attempts to emulate him went as far as deciding one summer between grade school years that I really was (along with Matt) Brad's younger brother, not his younger sister, and I took to wearing only boys' clothes. At the time there wasn't that big a difference between my clothes and my brothers' clothes, but when I say I wore only boys' clothes I mean right down to the white

Jockeys. Mary was aware of this and didn't say a word against it, nor did she make any remark when I got tired of wearing boys' underwear and went back to wearing my own.

All three of us were close, given that we mostly had each other as playmates when we weren't in school, but I knew I didn't completely fit into Brad's world. He told me one time that he and a friend were going to start a band called Dead on a Rifle, and even though I had no hope of being in the band, I thought it was a fantastic name—one that brought to mind a romantic picture of a poor cowboy who had died, somehow, right on top of his own gun. It wasn't until I saw the band's named shortened to D.O.A. that I knew I'd misunderstood something, but true to form, I did not ask what.

I had friends of my own, of course, but we lived far from town, and in the summer Pete and Mary were busy, and it wasn't always easy to get together with friends my age. I didn't have the companions they might've expected me to have, anyway, because I wasn't close friends with the cow-girls, meaning the girls who did horse 4-H and competed in high school rodeos in barrel racing and pole-bending. If I had a strength it was the fact that I was a straight-A student, and my friends were of that ilk. I was also pretty big on skiing, so I had friends there.

For some reason, Roy Reed seemed to be extra nice to me, maybe because I was the only girl on the ranch, by default the fifth wheel. He made me other things besides the horsehair wig, including Indian jewelry and feathered wall hangings. He was also a talented artist, and during the period in which I thought I wanted to be an artist, too, he gave me oil painting lessons in the living room of the old white house at the Double T. My artistic ambitions turned out to be short-lived, as I completed just one painting, but Roy Reed helped me every step of the way, with the little log cabin, with the wooded hillsides, the sky that he gently dissuaded me from painting a bright shade of turquoise. He also donated his oil paints, brushes, and even one of his large canvas boards, which I don't imagine were very easy to come by at that time and in that place.

In retrospect I don't suppose I wanted so much to learn how to paint as I wanted to have a piece of art to enter in the Teton County Fair, in the under-fourteen category. You'd think I would have entered categories having to do with horses or cattle, but as I said, I participated very little in 4-H and had an indifferent approach to barrel racing in junior high school. I was never going to try and be the Teton County Rodeo Queen or win a bunch of horse ribbons at the fair. This was probably because I didn't think I'd win them even if I did try, but it was also because I didn't think it seemed that much like fun.

As far as I was concerned, riding horses was a job, something you did in the course of work, because either you or your cows had to get from one location to another, and to this day I feel sheepish about riding horses when it doesn't involve getting a job done. It's not that I mind wasting my own time; it's just that I think the horse will know perfectly well if I'm wasting his.

So as far as the County Fair went, I was much more likely to get excited about entering an oil painting than I was about Western Pleasure. I did get an Honorable Mention ribbon for that painting, too, which I think approximated sixth place. Apparently this accolade didn't inspire me enough to continue painting, but Roy Reed did continue his drawing and painting and became very accomplished.

Brad and Matt and I, growing up, were captivated by Roy Reed's ability to draw. We would sometimes ask Roy Reed to illustrate specific things for us and he was always generous about complying. One evening in particular when he was babysitting us he offered to draw whatever we desired, by way of giving us each a gift. I don't remember what Brad and Matt's requests were, but I suppose they might have been Buck knives or race cars or something along those lines. I told Roy Reed that I would like him to draw me a city.

I wasn't very old at the time, but I'd been around long enough to have concluded that our family's circumstances must be pretty poor that we had to live in my great-grandmother's old log house out in the middle of a cow operation on a washboardy dirt road, and couldn't even walk to the drugstore. I believed that progress had cruelly passed us by—that while society might have advanced, our family had not. I believed that everyone who had a choice was living in cities and towns.

How wonderful I imagined it would be to reside where other people did, in the midst of stores and a movie theater and actual neighborhoods. I suspected, too, that because of my isolation—we didn't even have TV because it was prior to the advent of cable—I was missing out on important cultural references that I would never understand, things others would know innately.

I saw in the newspaper comics a man strong enough to rip a phone book in two, but our town was so small I could've done this myself. When I read the phrase "Go play in the street" in a book, I knew it was an insult, but because Spring Gulch Road wouldn't have posed a danger to anyone, this, too, made no sense to me. I knew that kids raised money with lemonade stands, but when Brad and Matt and I tried putting up an ice cream stand on Spring Gulch Road, our only customer was Pete as he drove out of the ranch gate, and we loaded his bowl past capacity before giving up and taking the melting ice cream back to the freezer.

I could only imagine that I was missing out on buckets of basic knowledge and experience that city kids were getting, and the worst part was, I'd probably never even know the extent of my ignorance. So when Roy Reed offered to draw anything I wanted, I asked for a city.

Roy Reed, without judging me, complied with my request. I didn't appreciate it at the time, but Roy Reed had probably not been to many cities much larger than the town of Jackson, population 3,000. I'm sure he'd been to Idaho Falls, Idaho, a town maybe ten times Jackson's size, about two hours away. There were stockyards in Idaho Falls if you needed to buy or sell a few cows, and there were stores with goods such as bath towels, dresses, and sheet music, specialty items you couldn't find in Jackson. But in spite of not being any better traveled than the rest of us, Roy Reed drew a nice illustration of a city, exactly what I'd hoped for.

It showed a main street lined with one-story buildings and storefronts arranged side by side around a single intersection. There was a sign over one of the store windows that read SHOES, which I found very appealing because there was no shoe store in Jackson at that time. You could buy cowboy boots, snow boots, and fishing waders, but nothing pretty. He drew the streets and buildings in perspective, as he had learned to do from his illustration books, and the effect was of a town that had been built rather low and wide instead of upwards. That didn't take anything away from it for me. I kept the drawing for several years, and it was a long time before I realized that it didn't represent much of a city, that it could have been any one of a dozen small Wyoming towns.

Roy Reed was artistic and sensitive, which I don't believe was either because of the way he was raised or in spite of the way he was raised; it was just his nature. From the time I was little I believed that people had mostly fixed natures, a notion I'd probably extrapolated from what I knew about animals. And if Roy Reed was inherently artistic and sensitive, his younger brother Will was on the side of fierce and impetuous.

Will seemed to have been born a cowboy as much as his older brother was born an Indian. Will was the first person I noticed who was a very good rider. I know my mother and father and any number of other people around me were good riders, too, but maybe because Will was my peer, I was truly struck by how differently he sat a horse than I did. I know the very day when it first hit me. One afternoon he'd ridden his dappled gray horse down to our house to visit with me, and I met him at the yard fence, out by the fire barrels. I thought it was unnecessary for him to have saddled and ridden his horse just to travel a mile because I always walked or rode my bike if I wanted to go up to Martins'. I thought it was even more unnecessary that he came down through the fields at a run, but then, I rarely saw Will ride anywhere, unless he was working cows, at anything less than a run.

I don't remember what Will had to say to me that afternoon, but from time to time he would come racing over to our house or call on the phone, apparently to speak to me but without really getting anywhere. Sometimes I got the feeling he was trying to impress me, but he remained mostly unknowable to me all the years I spent with him.

A group of us were riding through the West Field on a summer after-noon when he suddenly hopped off his horse, snatched a fat grasshopper out of the tall grass and put it alive into his mouth, chewing quickly. I thought there was a strong possibility, even when he asked if I wanted him to catch one for me, that he was doing it for show, and I declined his offer. But then he seemed to find the taste of the insect agreeable and maybe it was. Maybe Will ate grasshoppers when no one was around; I wouldn't doubt it.

Back to the day I realized what a good rider Will was: We probably didn't have much of a conversation, because I stayed on my side of the rail fence, on foot, and he was on the other side of it, on horseback. All I remember is that when he turned back toward the Double T with a forceful kick to his horse's gut, my eye was on the crown of his cowboy hat, and I noticed that as he tore up through the field on that running gray horse, the top of his hat stayed almost perfectly level, and it occurred to me that Will knew some things about riding horses that were beyond me.

Mary and Pete gave me essentially no formal instruction in riding. Instructions from my mother usually came in the form of "Go get the horses into the corral." In other words, what to do, unaccompanied by how, but I'm sure Will's parents didn't give him any formal instructions in horse riding, either. I'm sure he learned what he knew about riding horses mostly just by letting the miles go by, and there were miles and miles to pass under your stirrups when you were growing up on a cattle ranch. This seemed to be all it took for some people, if not for me.

Pete and Mary didn't object to my doing things poorly, anyway. What they objected to more was when I did things halfheartedly. My mother spoke with admiration one time of a dog I had, a real goer. "What I love about that dog," Mary said, "is that she never lets up on herself." Letting up on yourself was something my mother had so little regard for, she didn't even think dogs should do it.

The phrase "Get after it" was also one I heard often from my mother, and it didn't really matter what "it" was. Whether it was doing your work or having a good time, herding cattle or inner-tubing down the Gros Ventre River—she wasn't in favor of the lackadaisical approach.

She was particularly impatient with Brad, Matt, and me when we didn't control our horses. She thought it was foolish as well as dangerous for a rider to be unclear on who was in charge, and to let your horse do this or that as it pleased him—especially when his wishes didn't coincide with yours, but even when they did.

I was headed out onto the road in the snow very early one morning when my horse stopped at the ranch gate and refused to go farther. I don't remember the name of that horse, just that he was small and black and stubborn. Although we didn't often herd cattle in the winter, there was a bunch that apparently needed to go from one pasture to another, where there were still fresh haystacks, but I didn't have any idea about that. I was simply going along because I'd been told to, my brain essentially on autopilot.

But my horse balked at the gate and though I kicked him with my snow boots he wouldn't budge. Everyone else was on their way but he still wouldn't go, and in Mary's estimation that was because my efforts were a bit too delicate. The truth was, I didn't really want to go. It was bitterly cold that morning.

"Get after it," my mother said, and I did, but the horse was unconvinced. My mother had enough of that pretty shortly, and came up behind us and whipped him hard with her reins right next to his tail. He bucked me off at once and I landed on the gravel driveway on my back, like a sack of flour hitting the ground. The wind was knocked out of me and I was extremely surprised—I hadn't seen it coming at all—so just as soon as I was able to breathe, I started crying as loudly as possible.

Pete was angry with Mary for that and he scolded her right in front of everyone. At the time I thought it was because my horse had bucked and I'd landed hard, but later I found out that this was not what had upset him—it was the fact that she'd goosed the horse when it was right in front of that dangerous cattle guard. That morning, though, I thought it was about me, and I got some satisfaction from the idea that Pete was mad at Mary for getting me thrown off.

I could've easily stopped crying, actually; I wasn't hurt, and I expected that I'd get back on my horse just as my mother wanted me to after she hauled me up from the ground and whisked off the snow with her leather glove. But my father took my side and said that I didn't have to ride that day. So I took advantage of their disagreement and walked back to the house, making sure my continuing whimpers were audible to those behind me.

I didn't wonder, that day, if there might have been some way for me to ride it out, to not get bucked off in the first place. Naturally I had an objection to asking my mother or father exactly how a person went about riding a horse the way Will Martin rode a horse. Again, the standoff: They didn't say, and I didn't ask. For all I know my mother was actually waiting, full to the brim with helpful advice and observations—especially about riding horses—but would be forthcoming only if asked. Of course I had noticed that my parents, and my mother in particular, weren't usually overflowing with instructions, and maybe I concluded from this that I was supposed to have some instinctual knowledge about riding and ranch work—some inborn ability as part of my birthright—and if not, I shouldn't embarrass everyone by making that deficiency known.

So I forged my way ahead, pretending I could do things and hoping they would somehow come to me. And eventually, in spite of all my doubts, they began to. Maybe it was just a result of the literal and figurative miles going by, accumulating under my feet and in my brain as surely as they did for Will Martin, but somehow I got to the point where I stuck with a few of the ranch jobs long enough to learn how to do them well.

At that point I knew I was making a measurable contribution, and I knew that, like my parents, my brothers, and the ranch hands I so wanted to emulate, I was doing real work.

8

Real Work and a New Horse

WORK WENT ON YEAR-ROUND ON SPRING GULCH ROAD, BUT THE NATURE of the work itself underwent near-total transformations. The kind of work we did depended on the season and where we were in the cycle of a cow-calf operation. A particular job might go hard and fast every day for a while and then it would be done and halt completely. For me that was a good thing because I was short on patience; I liked it that when things were done, they were done, and many of them didn't have to be done again for another entire year.

Winter, the longest season in Wyoming, was relatively quiet. The cows were home from the range and had to be fed every morning, but that wasn't as much of a hurry-up job as branding or haying. It just seemed in winter that all the ranch inhabitants, the ranch hands as well as the animals, were moving more slowly and not going as far. (Ranchers in Wyoming used to let the cows forage over the winter like the elk did, but in the mid-1880s there was a winter that resulted in a loss of cattle so devastating that some people still refer to it as "the great die-off." After that a lot of cattle ranches shrunk in size and started growing hay to feed their cattle rather than making them dig through the snow.)

Until we bought the big new tractor when I was in junior high school, we used a team of draft horses to pull the hay wagon on runners over the snow-covered fields, with one man driving the team and one or two others balancing atop the pile of hay, pitching it off as they went. Sometimes, no one needed to drive the team. The Clydesdales could follow the same familiar circuit through the big pastures, if necessary, without needing a driver to work the lines, and all the hands could be up on top, pitching hay. The draft horses knew their own names—for instance, Chub and Shorty—and they responded to simple voice commands. And unlike a tractor, they wouldn't just run over an obstacle, such as a cow giving birth that was unable to get out of their way.

The workhorses were serious animals, and they didn't socialize much with the other horses or with us. I was a bit afraid to even give them a handful of grain in the corral because their oversize teeth and hooves struck me as potentially quite destructive. But they were steady and reliable and never seemed to fuss with their load, plodding out across the snow blowing steam. Ray was the one who broke the draft horses to pull the sleigh, and his method was efficient. He would hitch up a completely green horse in the harness next to an experienced one, and though the next few miles were pretty hard on the new horse, the old horse, and Ray, it didn't take long for the new horse to figure out what to do. He had little choice.

Usually snow was on the ground to stay by Halloween and still there at Easter when the calves were being born. The arrival of the white-faced newborns, not the calendar date of January first, was the beginning of the year for us. At that point things went from quiet to noisy, from still to hectic. Pete, Mary, and Roy Martin all took shifts as midwives, often through the night. If things appeared to be well with a new calf, which they usually were according to the hardy characteristics of Hereford cattle, they would simply get the calf ear-tagged with a number to match its mother's (although this could be hazardous, depending on how protective a temperament the cow happened to have). If the cow was having trouble with delivery, they would get it to the calving barn at the Double T and physically pull the calf by its soft little front hooves from the exhausted body of its mother. And if the calf was too cold or weak to get up and nurse, Mary would carry it back to the house and warm it with blankets and bottle-feed it. This usually worked liked magic within the space of mere hours, bringing the calf back to health.

I was never much help with calving because I was still in school that time of year. But one spring before I was old enough even for kindergarten,

Matt and I had the job of bottle-feeding an orphan that Mary was keeping in our fenced yard, and it became very attached to Matt and me, or at least, to our milk bottle. When we came outside one morning without the bottle the calf prodded us both aggressively with its rubbery, wet nose. Rather than just going back in the house we ran away, and consequently it chased us. Although I enjoyed feeding the calf, I didn't like it running after me, and I ran faster. So did Matt. Finally we were dashing around the perimeter of the yard at top speed with the little devil at our heels, unable to shake it, hollering at my mother for help.

The calf had grown quite healthy on its bottle-fed diet and it could've easily outrun us. But it didn't want to outrun us; it just wanted us to give it a bottle. So it stayed right with us, and no matter how fast or slowly I ran it seemed to remain an inch behind me. When my mother saw what was happening, she had the presence of mind to take a movie of it with her Super 8 camera, which is one reason I remember this incident so vividly. At the time I laughed along with everyone else when we watched the movie, even though I didn't actually think it was that funny. I took myself quite a bit more seriously than how I looked in the film.

Other than that especially assertive calf, though, I loved the little things, and I worried about them. My own reaction every year was that they were being born too soon—that we must've accidentally trucked the bulls up to the summer range too early—that we'd surely lose half the newborns in the snowstorms of March and April. Though undoubtedly they would've had it easier if they'd been born in May, the calves had to be strong enough by the first days of summer that they could make it all the way to the range on federal land, so their arrival was planned with this in mind.

I felt especially sorry for the calves that, despite my mother's expert and attentive midwifery, didn't make it in the spring. And I was sickened when my mother, returning from her rounds one morning, reported that she'd found a newborn calf who'd been too weak to get up and nurse. He'd had his ears eaten off during the night by a coyote, chewed and torn all the way down to his little head. My mother was as hurt over this as I was, and she cursed the mother cow who hadn't run the coyote off, the coyote who'd been so bold, and coyotes in general. Although the calf survived the disfigurement, coyotes for me had a black mark by their name from that day forward.

My mother didn't seem to worry too much if it was snowing on the new calves, but she feared the cold spring rains almost as much as the coyotes. The calves could take the cold temperatures if they were eating, but they seemed to be drained of all energy if they got wet. Once their skin was soaked it was hard for them to stay warm, and that's when they were susceptible to sickness. Inevitably Mary lost a few calves and a few mothers; when the mothers died, she had to work quickly to make sure the calves were cared for.

A trick she and Pete used was to skin a dead calf and tie that hide to the back of a calf whose mother had died giving birth. Most of the time, the mother who'd lost her calf was fooled into thinking that this new one belonged to her, which made bottle-feeding, at least for that baby, unnecessary.

One way or another, Mary, Pete, and Roy mothered all thousand head of cows through the ritual of calving every year with a soft voice and a gentle hand, and before I knew it, nearly all the cows had done their duty and the fields were teeming with clean new calves, and somehow, the snow had melted too. And then before long we were branding.

A day of branding began with riding, an early-morning gathering of the cows and calves, followed by some quick sorting in the corrals to separate the mothers from their offspring, and that's when the noise started. The calves called for their mamas, and vice versa, some mothers so devoted they went hoarse during the two or three hours in which they might be separated from their babies.

When I was little we didn't have calf tables—contraptions that work like a chute, except that one side of it pins the calf with curved metal tubes and then flips up horizontally, so the calf is lying on its one side, ready to be branded on the other. The calf tables make branding much easier, but in the very early days of my branding experience, the cowboys roped the calves one by one in the dirt corral and we just held them down on the ground. My father taught Brad and me how to grip their hind legs just above the hooves and brace our boot against their bottoms so they couldn't kick us to death while they got the once-over.

We almost always branded on Saturdays or Sundays so that my brothers and I would not have to miss school to help. We worked side by side: my dad, my mom, my two brothers, and me, along with ranch hands and sometimes a few volunteers from town. With two calf tables, we could brand at more than double the rate of the roping and wrestling method, meaning nearly a hundred calves an hour. This was an orchestrated effort that only worked if everyone involved knew exactly where they were supposed to be, and when. Keeping up that kind of pace is pretty remarkable when you consider that branding doesn't just mean marking each calf with the iron—it means branding, de-horning, vaccinating, ear-tagging, castrating, and dewlapping.

Dewlapping is cutting a thin flap of skin from a calf's throat, so that it hangs down like the dewlap, or waddle, that a moose comes by naturally. When I was little I watched Pete dewlapping without knowing why in the world he would do such a thing. He'd drag his pocketknife carefully down the length of a sharpening stone, making it shine, and I'd watch as he pulled the neck hide away and inserted the knife to cut the skin and nothing else, drawing very little blood, to create a dewlap.

Later I learned that a dewlap is a differentiating mark that, unlike a brand, can be seen from far away and from either side. Our cattle shared the summer range with other ranches in the Bacon Creek Association, so dewlaps helped the herder and others identify whose was whose more easily, because not every ranch would dewlap. But I watched Pete do it for years before asking the rationale, and for me it was in the same category as quite a few other things: a job that had to be done whether or not it made sense to me, even if it seemed bizarre.

No one took any pleasure in hurting the calves, but even I had clarity on what the purpose was, so I steeled myself to branding and all that it entailed early on. Since our cows summered with other herds we had to be able to tell who belonged to whom when they came home in the fall. They grazed so far up the Gros Ventre River in the summer, forty miles upstream from the ranch where we lived, that they could conceivably have wandered as far east as Dubois, where a quick consultation with the Wyoming Brand Book would tell any honest person who owned them.

I didn't really have to hurt the calves myself, anyway. Pete had me cut a dewlap one time, but as I felt the knife separating the hide at the little calf's throat I was uncomfortable with what was at stake and my hand was unsteady, and I didn't cut it smoothly. That didn't disqualify me from having another try, in Pete's opinion, but it did in my own, and I didn't take up the knife again. My jobs were almost always vaccinating and ear-tagging, which were painless procedures compared to everything else our calves were subjected to in their ninety seconds on the table. I was just there to give them a little shot so they didn't get sick and an earring so they didn't get lost. I made sure my syringe had no air bubbles and that I inserted it as gently as possible under the hide alongside their ribs before injecting the serum. I patted them afterwards, letting myself think that this was a comfort to them. Although I was careful I did both vaccinating and ear-tagging as quickly as I could, and I noticed that this was everyone else's approach, too. Do it right, but get it over with and move on to the next one.

It looked to me like there was nothing harder on the calves than de-horning, which required pushing and twisting the cylindrical iron, red with heat, onto the little nubs of horn just beginning to surface beside their ears. I found out at one point that you could de-horn a cow with a dab of paste instead of with a hot iron, and I asked Mary why we didn't use what was obviously a more humane method.

So Mary described to me the holes she'd seen in the heads of calves who'd been treated with the paste, maggots crawling in their wounds. She told about watching another rancher's calf backing up and backing up in the field, shaking its head as if it were deranged, trying to get away from the chemical boring into its head. Quick, severe pain is always better than long, slow torture, my mother said.

After branding the big job was getting the cows to the range, and once that was done we settled into summer. For a brief time it always seemed we could relax a bit. Ray and Roy would be irrigating the hayfields, but until the grass was grown high and ready to be mowed, there wasn't that much for my brothers and me to do. School was out, and during the short space of that breather was when we did most of our non-work enterprises, such as fixing up our fort in the rafters, and practicing our driving.

My brothers and I learned to drive pretty early, as did most ranch kids, and I sometimes had the opportunity to teach my friends how to operate motor vehicles, too. I usually dispensed my expertise out in the hayfields where we didn't have to worry about other traffic, or even staying on the road.

My friend Kathy wanted driving lessons in junior high, and on an afternoon when Mary and Pete weren't home I took her out in the ranch pickup and showed her how to operate the gearshift and the clutch over the course of about half a mile. Having demonstrated that I moved to the passenger side and let her take over. I hadn't thought the operation of the steering wheel needed any explanation, and I was truly surprised when Kathy turned the truck off the side of a plank bridge, landing us in Spring Creek.

Pete and Mary were surprised, too, when they flew over the ranch in their small plane a few hours later and saw the blue pickup sitting down in the creek, water running around it. There really hadn't been anything I could do about it. There was no way for Kathy and me to get the truck either driven or hauled out of the creek bed, so we'd just killed the engine, hopped out into the water, and waded to shore. We only had to walk about half a mile down through the fields to get back to the house.

What Pete found most interesting about it, he said later, was that both pickup doors, which he and my mother could see clearly from the air, were left hanging open. They weren't mad at me for driving the pickup, or even for letting one of my bungling friends drive it while they were gone. But when Pete remarked, "I guess when you decide to walk off, you walk off," I did wish I had shut the doors.

Pete and Mary didn't let us drive because it was fun for us or our friends, though. It was because they needed for us to know how to drive. The first paycheck I ever got on the ranch was for driving, and it was $33.00, my entire summer's earnings. The job I had at that time was bringing water to the hay crew. At age ten, I was allowed to take my mother's manual-transmission Volkswagen out into the fields with jugs of water and paper cups for the refreshment of those who were doing the hard work in the dust and heat of the hayfields.

I preferred to drive the pickup even though it was quite a stretch to the pedals, but I used my mother's Volkswagen to take water to the ranch hands during haying season because the ranch pickup was needed by others for more important work. I believe my pay was set at a dollar a day for carrying water, which was more than fair considering that the hardest and highest-paid workers—those in the haystack itself, pitching each load into the corners as the hay toppled down over them—got ten dollars a day.

Apparently I didn't get my water delivered every day because I know haying season lasted more than thirty-three days. But there were jugs of water where the stack was going up anyway, and the only people who really had any use for my services were those driving the buck rakes some distance from the stack yard, gathering up the cut hay to bring to the stack. And even the buck rake drivers could have pulled over at the stack yard anytime they wanted to get a drink.

So I knew even then that Mary and Pete were drumming up a job for me, one that wasn't normally on the payroll, and one that could be undertaken not in a working vehicle but in a Volkswagen. I took the job anyway because I wanted the money, and working was the only way to get it. My mother didn't hand out money readily. Not money and not things. She didn't want any of us to go through life thinking it was just fine to go ahead and let your cousin's old shoe go through the culvert and down the creek—that, oh well, you could just get another pair.

I made a lot more money when I was finally old enough to drive a tractor at the age of twelve. The tractor I got to know best was a Farmall Super C that had been manufactured in the early fifties, but was such a simple thing to operate, maintain, and fix that it was still going strong in the seventies when I was driving it. My job was to turn the rows of cut hay over so they could dry on both sides before being picked up and added to the stack. In the right weather they could dry in less than a day, and then I'd drive the rows again that afternoon to combine them, cutting the job of the buck rake drivers—who came along later to scoop up the rows—in half.

I don't really like to think of myself as someone who's well suited to repetitive tasks, but I was perfectly happy driving a tractor, pulling a side-delivery rake up and down, back and forth, one row after another, and then on to the next field where I repeated the process. Acre after acre, field after field, row after row. There weren't a lot of surprises and I had no company, which agreed with me.

We did have a dog in high school who sometimes ran along beside me. One summer there was a coyote pup that came out to inspect our proceedings, and Missie, the dog, took after it. She was an athletic dog and put in quite a few miles living on a cattle ranch, but she was no match for the coyote. It didn't seem to want to get away from her, though, because it ran in big circles. And when Missie was forced to lie down and catch her breath the odd little coyote sat down too, about twenty yards away, and waited for her. Then up and away they would go.

That incident sticks out because it was one of the very few times I had any entertainment while driving a tractor. I watched the hawks and ravens going after field mice, but other than that I was obliged to entertain myself. I made up songs and sang them as loudly as I had a mind to. No one could hear me, and in fact, I couldn't hear myself above the noise of the Super C.

But I did a good job, and gradually that became clear to me. I wasn't the only person dragging a side-delivery rake in the summer; there was too much hay on too much ground for one person to keep up with it. And according to Pete, who wasn't reckless in handing out compliments, I was the best raker on the place. His compliment changed the way I approached it. Once I knew how good I supposedly was, it became my mission not to leave so much as a handful of hay outside its row, and I really looked forward to the times when Pete drove out to my field in his pickup to check if my hay was ready for stacking. I knew he'd see as he looked around that my rows were neat and my fields clean.

He asked me a few times to teach other hired hands how to rake, and there was one from the East Coast who had a problem with my being his instructor. He was a nice person but he'd come out to the ranch through a skiing connection because he wanted to spend the summer doing man's work. He was somewhat dismayed, when he arrived, to find that a teenage girl was going to tell him not only how to drive the tractor and get the hay raked, but also how to grease the tractor joints, check the oil, and spray ether into the carburetor if he couldn't get his machine started. As for me I was dismayed to find this backward point of view coming from someone from the East Coast who I would have assumed was my intellectual superior.

Working at that level gave me proprietary feelings about the hay I raked. Sometimes the elk would come down from the mountains in the winter and avail themselves of what we'd irrigated, harvested, and stacked to keep our cattle alive. One January day when I saw some elk in a stack yard at the Bar B C, I complained, thinking about how hard I'd worked the summer before on the hay crew, and I asked why somebody didn't go run them off. But even Mary was circumspect about ranching in some ways, and she didn't seem too worried about it.

"Oh, well," she said, gazing out the pickup truck window at the animals who were so much more elegant than our cattle, and every bit as hungry. "They were here before we were."

My mother's haying job was driving the winch, which was basically a reconfigured pickup truck that didn't go anywhere under its own power but had to be towed from one stack yard to another. Pete was a good mechanic, and also creative. He had disconnected the drive shaft of that pickup so that the engine powered two steel drums. The drums spooled the cables that ran the pole basket up and down the beaver slide, dumping loads of hay into the thirty-foot fences of the stack yard. The basket sat at the bottom of the slide waiting for the buck rakes to come and unload their piles of loose hay, which they did about every twenty seconds. Then my mother would put the winch in gear, picking up the slack in the cables, and give it some gas, causing the steel drums to wind the cable and hoist the fifteen-foot pole basket up the slide. As the cables whipped through the pulleys at the top of the slide, the pole basket ran up the 45-degree wooden slats, slowly or lickety-split, depending on precisely where my mother intended to place the load of hay.

She made it look easy but it wasn't, and very few people did it well. If you ran the basket up too fast, you could break the top pulleys right off the slide and kill someone with the falling basket. In fact, one of our ranch hands did launch the basket into the stack one time, and although he was lucky enough not to kill any of the stackers, he did break another ranch hand's arm.

Letting the basket come down the slide also required careful skill. If you let it back down without braking at the exact right moment, the cables could snap at the bottom and the basket would go flying out into the meadow, which could potentially have been a hazard to even more people on the ground. And your timing with the clutch made all the difference in how quickly or slowly the hay dropped out of the basket onto the top of the stack, and how much area you covered.

Mary's finesse with this crude piece of cobbled-together machinery lessened the workload for the stackers, the four hands with pitchforks who were standing inside the stack yard itself, filling the corners for ten dollars a day. It also meant that stacking progressed quickly. Our old-fashioned loose stacks held about twenty tons of hay, and on a good day the crew could put up half a dozen of them—120 tons.

In July and August I was on the hay crew myself, but in September I had to go back to school. After I got home from school on those afternoons when haying was still under way, I would always run out to wherever they'd moved the stack yard—since I could usually see it from the house even if it was a mile away—and watch the work. Mary let me sit on the barrel gas tank next to where her seat was on the winch, and I can clearly recall the way my mother muscled the gearshift and revved the accelerator, and the fragments of conversation we'd have between loads as I got her caught up on my day.

Mary was tanned in the summer and muscular for a slight woman. She wore sunglasses rather than a cowboy hat when she was haying, and she was pretty. She'd come home from the fields at night with her hair full of hayseed and her nostrils full of dust. When I saw her at work I could tell that she was giving it all she had, free of self-doubt, just as she had from the time she was a little girl, and as I watched her I felt keenly that even when my own work on the hay crew merited a paycheck, I was probably not operating at her level.

It was a new horse that changed my status, even more than the fact that I'd done a good job with the tractor driving.

When I was little my horses were chosen mostly for their temperament and predictability, as a matter of safety. Their ability to perform was a secondary consideration. But then I finally got a horse who was interested enough in what we were doing to join in my efforts, rather than do this or that just because I might make him. This gave me higher expectations as to whether or not my presence on horseback could make any real difference to our work with cattle—the real core of our business. This carried more weight than driving a tractor, because haying was secondary; we only grew and stockpiled hay to take care of our cattle.

When I was in sixth grade and needed a horse, rather than saying, "Muffy might as well ride so-and-so" as she usually did, my mother drove me over to a large horse ranch in Ashton, Idaho, one fall to see what they were selling. There was one little horse, not even weaned from his mother, who caught my eye at first just because of his coloring. He was a rich buckskin with a black mane and tail, but although his legs and hooves were dark, he had a little swath of white above each hoof, and a couple of bright white strokes on his face which made him particularly special looking. He also stood out because of the way he held his head up high as he ran on his mother's flank across the fall stubble in the Ashton pastures, throwing his legs out in front of him and kicking up dust in the bare spots.

I stood there at the fence with Mary, both of us apparently drawn to the same horse from among the hundred or more in the herd. At the time I thought the fact that she asked the breeder to bring in the very horse I'd identified as being the best-looking one in the pasture was a startling coincidence, because I knew I was no judge of horses, and I didn't think she'd really let me choose a horse for our ranch when it would be her money that paid for him. But she bought him for me, and we brought the buckskin home in the back of the pickup that day, alongside a three-year-old gelding my mother had picked out for herself. I felt so sorry for him when I listened to the little horse forget his pride and whinny, as we went up and over Teton Pass, for the mother he would never see again.

I named him Dusty, and we started getting to know each other in the winter that followed when I pitched hay to him in the mornings before school. He wasn't nearly old enough for me to ride him that winter, but still there was a bond that came with meeting up every morning in the corral, whether it was snowing, blowing, or doing both full bore. He looked forward to his breakfast, but I could tell he looked forward to seeing me, too. He usually wanted to play. He was never a horse who would bite people, but he liked to take my ski hat off my head and toss it behind him and watch me go pick it up.

Then when he was old enough for me to ride and train him, he took an interest in cows. He seemed to understand as innately as a shepherd dog the importance of keeping them gathered up, but he was also quick to grasp which one it was you were trying to cut out from the herd when you needed to. He never balked at thick willows, at rushing streams, or at a steep, muddy bank. The only thing he didn't like very well was ice, and he'd walk across it almost as if on tiptoe.

But it wasn't just the fact that Dusty was smarter and more athletic than my previous horses had been. We'd met when he was a baby, and as I was coming into a sense of myself. And so we grew together and got to where we knew each other well. I often believed that I knew what he was thinking, and to some extent, I'm certain this went both ways. This horse and I connected, and in the end I think I learned more about riding horses from Dusty than from anyone else.

9

Riding Up from the Drag

WE MOVED CATTLE AROUND VARIOUS PASTURES ON THE RANCH AT TIMES when they were home during the winter, or when we sorted them for branding or weaning, but once in the spring and once in the fall we had our principal cattle drive, one that took four days. It was the only practical way to get our cattle to and from their summer range, forty miles above the ranch.

I didn't like the fall cattle drive quite as well as the spring. For one thing, the fall drive meant the long Wyoming winter was upon us. For another, it was much more difficult to gather our cows when they were scattered among the gullies and hillsides and creek drainages of their vast summer range than it was to gather them from the confines of our own property for the spring drive.

The fall drive started in the wandering gray hills of the Bacon Creek Range above the Dew Place and ended—fences and civilization encroaching mile by mile as we went downstream—in the narrow confines of Spring Gulch Road.

Dusty sometimes started the fall gathering out of sorts, too; as soon as I got him out of the stock truck I'd be able to tell if he was going to try and buck me off, and quite often he did have that on his mind. He was never deterred by the fact that he hadn't succeeded in bucking me off since I was twelve years old and had first started riding him regularly. I hadn't anticipated it that day, and once I let him get his head down between his front legs he'd sent me over his withers quite easily; he humped his back up and popped me off with one jump. I'd somersaulted just enough to land on my shoulder blades and my back was sore for a month, so I did everything possible after that not to repeat my performance.

Dusty tried to repeat his, however, on more than one of those frosted mornings when we started gathering cattle for the trip home. He would let me get into the saddle all right and wait until I started kicking him before he made his objection known. Initially he might oppose me by simply refusing to move, ignoring my exertions, whereupon I would kick him more forcefully and probably say some foul words. Or he would oppose me by wanting to race off after everyone else when I was holding him back, steering in a different direction. Either way, at that point he'd feel justified in actually trying to pitch me off, and if he wanted to, he could buck pretty hard. Later in his life he broke my father's pelvis just by bucking, even though Pete didn't get thrown; his injury came by virtue of sticking with the horse.

It wasn't like Dusty would just spring it on you for no reason, though, and of course it's easier to stay on when you know it's coming, and he usually didn't put that much effort into it. After he'd given me a few good hops as he fought with me to get his head down and his back up, he'd usually resign himself to our work and get on with it. He liked herding cattle, but sometimes it seemed like he wanted everything to be his idea. Or maybe it was just more exercise than he thought he needed, hoofing it up and down the hilly ground around Bacon Creek looking for the odd pocket of cows in the freezing cold. In any case, by the time we got back to the ranch four days later Dusty was pretty much bombproof, just as tired as I was.

I liked the spring drive better. Though you can't always count on June being summery in northwest Wyoming, the weather was bound to be better than it was in October. And it was a relief not to worry, as we did when we gathered cows off the range to come home, about whether or not we'd left anyone behind. Once I'd heard the story about Pete's Christmastime trek to the Dew Place, it was always on my mind.

But in the springtime gathering was easy. We collected up our entire herd from within the confines of our own fences and funneled them through our gates out onto Spring Gulch Road, turning them north.

During the years when we pastured them on the Bacon Creek Range in Grand Teton National Forest, they had four days of uphill walking ahead of them before they reached the high summer pastures above the Dew.

I didn't get paid for cowboying—I only got paid for my haying job—but I didn't care. Much as I disliked the fact that I usually ended up at the back of the herd, the drag, I would have hated being left behind on those twice-yearly pilgrimages up to the range in the spring and then home to the ranch in the fall. Once I thought I had the hang of herding cattle I loved it, and I loved it even more after I got Dusty. As I said, he was the kind of horse who had ideas of his own about the job in front of us. I could tell, especially when we were gathering cows in the fall on the rough terrain of the Bacon Creek Range, that he wasn't just waiting for me to spot them and turn him in their direction; he was on the lookout for strays himself. He was sometimes watching even more carefully than I was, but if I saw the cow first he was quick to respond to my signals. Unlike my childhood horses, he'd get going without making you flap your legs like bird wings.

The four-day journey from our ranch to the Dew Place, which was where we entered into the Bacon Creek Range, took us over forty miles of all kinds of country. Most of the trip we were far removed from society, but on the first day as we went up Spring Gulch Road we sometimes had to work around a little traffic—or maybe I should say it had to work around us. When we crossed the highway that took tourists up into Grand Teton National Park and further into Yellowstone, the cars would get stacked up, sometimes dozens on each side, as we crossed with the herd. The people never seemed to be annoyed by the delay we'd caused them; on the contrary, many of them got out of their vehicles and took pictures.

I'm sure that for many visitors to Wyoming, the fact that they got waylaid in the middle of a cattle drive authenticated their whole trip west. But at the time I was a little worried that we might be quaint, or simply oddities, which I'm sure had everything to do with the fact that I was ambivalent about our family's circumstances in the first place. We were stuck in a died-out century, I thought, with our weathered buildings, our old machinery, my mother's clothesline, and our antique way of making a living. And there we were, trying to make a living in front of all these people who were just on vacation, whose living-room slide shows we'd eventually be a part of.

There was almost always a little bit of hurried cowboying at the highway because, as we approached the crossing, one or more of the cows would usually get spooked by people with cameras and break from the herd, running off into the borrow pit toward town, or maybe thinking they'd skip back to the ranch. When that happened you just crossed your fingers that one of the tourists didn't get it in his mind to help you, because the fundamentals of herding cattle didn't seem intuitive to them.

People didn't seem to understand that, to cows, any shouted voice command means "Run!" In other words, you couldn't yell at a cow to stop or turn. A cow will almost never change her course as long as you're right on her tail. I was always amazed at the way my mother, acting, it seemed, as personal ambassador for the cattle industry, graciously shouted "Thank you! Good morning! Thank you!" as she galloped by one of the tourists on her way to round up the cow he had inadvertently chased the wrong way down the highway.

Will Martin told me how a tourist stopped him once to ask a few remarkable questions, including, as he gestured at the herd, "What do you feed them?"

"They catch chiselers," is what Will told me he answered, and according to him the tourist swallowed it whole. I can believe somebody asked that question but I didn't believe Will really answered that way—nor does it seem plausible that the tourist would have known that "chiseler" was our word for ground squirrel. I just understood that it was part of the running commentary we had among ourselves on how ill-informed the tourists seemed to be, no matter how obvious the evidence, such as cattle eating grass right on the side of the highway not thirty feet from them. It was satisfying, not just to Will but to me, too, to speak in disdainful terms about the tourists, especially when you believed they were far more sophisticated than you were.

After we crossed that highway at midday we were less than a mile from our first night's stop. If we were herding cows and calves they would have all afternoon to mother-up and rest, and as soon as we stopped pushing them along they got to that business. Hundreds of mothers and hundreds of babies bawled for each other all at the same time and it was a wonder to me that they ever sorted themselves out. Everyone went back to the ranch to sleep that night except for Pete and a few others who stayed behind with saddled horses to make sure the cattle didn't decide to turn back while we slept. The rest of us would show up at about four o'clock the next morning to get them gathered, and started up the road again in the dark.

At the beginning of the spring cattle drive we were often on roads that actually had fences on both sides, which made herding pretty easy, but after the first day we were on public lands and the fences became scarcer. As we rode up the Gros Ventre drainage to the summer range, the surroundings redrew themselves with every mile. First the people dropped away. We didn't see too many cars once we crossed the park highway and left whatever tumult we'd created with the tourists behind us. Then the buildings became extremely sparse. I looked for the slight structures of the town of Kelly, Wyoming, for a long time before I could actually get a glimpse of them.

And then finally as we made our way up the country through the changing colors of dirt, past red mountains, then gray ones, the fences themselves became a rarity, and I felt I was somewhere older than the Old West, a place that hadn't changed essentially for not just hundreds but for thousands of years. I'd been aware since elementary school that I was going uphill as I went upstream, but riding up the Gros Ventre River I felt like I was also going back in time, regressing with every mile into our community's past, before Westerners had much in the way of machines or luxuries. And although I was enthralled by the landscape, even more than I understood at the time, I traveled with some reluctance too, as I felt myself riding away from the civilized world I'd always wanted to inhabit.

The Dew Place seemed to me about as far away as Montana at the time—partly because it took four days of riding, and partly because we crossed over such a variety of terrain. The changing color of the dirt as we went up the river was almost as stark to me as all the other milestones. I probably spent too much time looking down at dirt but it interested me, the way it changed. It was just regular brown in Spring Gulch, but by the time we got halfway to the Bar Double R it had turned rusty red, and up toward the Dew Place it turned the same light gray as the cliffs bordering the Gros Ventre River up above the Bar Double R. I didn't know much about geology, but I marked our progress with the changes in the dirt color along with the other old, familiar landmarks.

The small encampment of Kelly, which we passed by on the second day, had a general store and was the one place on the cattle drive where we could stop and maybe buy a pack of gum. By the time we got to Kelly we'd made it past the federal government's alfalfa fields and could relax a bit. After I'd seen one cow die of alfalfa bloat I was skittish riding through that corridor, and always gave a warm mental greeting to the west side of Kelly. One side of Kelly was only a few hundred feet from the other, but it was a major milestone nonetheless, and the only town you went through on your way up the Gros Ventre.

There is a hot springs just above Kelly where the steam rises so thick you can't see to the other side on a cold morning, and we would sometimes find that someone had pitched a tent there. It wouldn't have been someone we would know, not someone from around there, but maybe someone whose VW bus had California license plates on it. Regardless of where they were from, the people in the tent were never awake at five o'clock in the morning. We'd hope the tent itself wouldn't spook the cattle and that we could get on by without too much of a disturbance for either side.

We rode later that same day past three-mile-long Slide Lake, formed in 1925 when fifty million cubic yards of mountainside collapsed across the Gros Ventre River, creating a natural dam very suddenly, and then more gradually, a lake. That lake has always given me an eerie feeling when I go by it, because the bleached skeletons of many dead trees still stick out of the shallows at its upper end, and much of the pared-down mountainside is still so raw it looks like the cataclysm just occurred.

Two years after the collapse of the mountainside there had been another cataclysm when the natural slide-dam washed out, a disaster for the fledgling town of Kelly, which my grandfather remembered well. He told me the story and it's the story I still think about when I go up past Kelly and Slide Lake above it.

Charlie Dibble, a forest ranger who lived in Kelly, was keeping an eye on the earthen dam. Although different people had made predictions about it, the US Army Corps of Engineers, along with other geologists and scientists, had said it would never go out. Still, Charlie was watching it pretty closely. On May 17, 1927, he looked up from where he was removing debris from the Kelly Bridge, caused by the high runoff of water, and he saw a hayrack coming down the river.

After driving his little Model T up the road to get a better look, he confirmed that the natural dam had been breached and the water of Slide Lake was coming. He turned around and dashed to Kelly to warn everyone that they had fifteen minutes to clear out for higher ground. According to my grandfather, one man who had a little gristmill that took advantage of the water power refused to leave.

"If the flood takes my mill I want to go with it," he'd said, and dropped out of the group on foot. Charlie Dibble tried to save the man's little son but he got away and ran back to his father and mother. They were among the six people killed in the flood that day, and a few days later, they found the little boy's body on our ranch, ten miles downstream.

Partly as a consequence of being decimated by the flood, Kelly was passed over as county seat and never became much of a town. But every time we rode by Kelly and I thought about the wall of water going through, I pictured not so much the people who knew what was coming and could make up their own minds about whether to stay or go, but the livestock unable to escape their fenced pastures. Hundreds of them were lost that day.

I've always been fond of cows, and I've always believed they are smart even though I've heard some people say the opposite is true. I've observed that they have personalities, too. Posy the milk cow was as sweet as could be, but some of the Herefords, especially if they'd not yet had a calf of their own, could act a little nutty. Either way, they were entrusted to our care, and I took my cue from the way my mother would speak to a young cow when she maneuvered it into a stall in the calving barn to help it give birth for the first time.

"It's okay, mama," she'd say to the cow, in a voice filled with gentle sympathy (and more, I noticed, than she usually had for me). "You're a good mama," she'd say, and those who were good mothers could look forward to a long life, sometimes twenty years or more, under Mary and Pete's stewardship.

We got to know some of those long-timers quite well, and a few of them even had names. But the hundreds who didn't have names weren't usually referred to as "it." Instead we said, "She's got a sore foot, poor gal," or "He just needs to find his mama." I picked up on that, and one day on the drive to the range, I asked Mary, "Who is that calf?" I was pointing to a dappled orange calf who stuck out, walking in a bunch that had regular dark-red Hereford coloring.

Mary laughed at my wording, but answered, "That's Roany's calf." Roany was one of her longtime favorite cows, one with so much white hair mixed into her Hereford hide that she looked almost peachy-orange, as did most of her calves, year after year.

I believe my mother thought as highly of the cows as I did, though I don't know that she sang to them the way I did. As I've already confessed, I liked to sing quite a bit when I was young, but only when I thought no one could hear me. I would stand in the window of the hayloft in the horse barn and sing out into the air above the corral, bits and pieces of real songs sometimes, and more often romantic notions I thought up about myself and my life set to whatever tune came to me as I looked out across the buildings and the sweeps of pasture and all the way over to West Gros Ventre Butte. When there were cows in the adjacent pasture they could hear me, and, as if entranced, they'd stop eating, collect themselves, and walk a hundred yards to the corral, gathering wide-eyed below the hayloft window, gazing up at me in what appeared to be sincere wonderment. They'd stand there as a group listening for as long as I'd keep singing. I assumed my songs sounded as beautiful to them as they did to me, or that my voice must have had some unique quality that drew animals in from the far reaches of the pasture.

In any case, I took it as proof of their intelligence that they would want to stop eating just to listen to music. So I could never ride through Kelly without thinking of the cows trapped by barbed-wire fences as a lake of water bore down on them, without wondering who they might've been.

Even riding on the drag I had a few adventures and the recollection of one in particular gives me a shiver. At the end of the second day on our way to the range we would cross the Gros Ventre River at the bridge, and even if there were riders stationed on both flanks we usually had some cattle peel off to the sides, especially when going upriver, because by the time the cattle got to the crossing they were eager for water. One spring when I was in high school and we were headed up the Gros Ventre, I'd already crossed the bridge when up ahead of me, I saw three cows drop off the road and down the steep bank to go for a drink. The muddy river was running high along the bank, and fast, and I wanted to get them just two miles farther up to Crystal Creek where the ground and the river spread out flatter and it would be safer to get to water.

The bank between the road and river was so steep a person couldn't stand still on it, but cows with their split, pointy hooves are amazingly sure-footed. As sure-footed as Dusty was himself, I didn't want to risk him falling down that steep bank so I left him at the road and picked my way down on foot, grabbing at the trunks of the pine trees to keep from skiing in my boots as I clumsily scrambled down. I knew I could count on Dusty to stand and wait for me to come back up after I'd spooked the cows. When I got to the bank I could see that the three cows were just upriver from me in swift brown water up to their shoulders, with their hindquarters mostly on the steep bank out of the water, and I thought it might be pretty easy to shoo them back up to the road.

I had on leather gloves and grabbed hold of a long, stickery pine branch and leaned out across the water, hollering at the cows, hoping my voice would get around them since I couldn't. They pulled their noses out of the drink and looked up at me with a surprised expression on their faces as my branch broke, and I plunged into the deep muscle of the cold river and was off downstream, moving fast away from my cows and my horse both.

My brother had invited his team-roping partner Kevin Gattis to ride with us that day, and he partly saw and partly heard what had happened from where he sat in his saddle up at the road. I hurtled down with the flow, trying to swim in my cowboy boots. There I was in the same cold river, at about the same time of year, that had sent a whole hayrack bobbing into the town of Kelly. I wondered where I'd stop.

I had no problem keeping my head above water. In fact it was shallow enough where I was, not that far from the bank, that my boots could skip along the bottom at wide intervals, but it was running so fast that I was making slow, or no, progress to the bank and excellent progress downriver. The river got considerably steeper, faster, and rougher about half a mile below there, I knew, and I felt some urgency about getting the hell out of it.

I could hear the shod hooves of a horse galloping full tilt down the hard road above me, going faster than I was, and after a few minutes I came to Kevin's strong arm sticking out from the bank, and I was able to grab his hand, wet leather to dry, and stick. He was tall and powerful, and he yanked me out of the water in a wink, for which I was extremely grateful, not wanting to wash up in Slide Lake. I was also happy about the fact that it was late in the morning and warm, because the only way to dry off was to keep going. Not that much earlier it had been only thirty-some degrees outside. So I walked back up the road to my horse, and I truly believe he was glad to see me.

Mary and Pete would've been glad to see me safely out of the river, too, I'm sure, but by the time I saw them again I was dried out, and the importance of the incident itself had also evaporated, and I figured that telling them about it after the fact would come off as a ploy for sympathy, so as far as I knew they never heard about it.

At the place where Kevin pulled me from the river we'd just ridden past the Bar Double R, our summer place, which was indeed accessible only in the summer unless you were on snowmobiles. Once we got the cows settled just above Crystal Creek we would ride the couple of miles back to the Bar Double R and spend the night there. It was a luxury to be able to stay in our own beds there; it meant we didn't have to drive twenty miles back down to the Lower Ranch, and, more important, didn't have to drive the twenty miles back upriver before sunrise the next morning to get the herd going again.

As I said, I usually rode with the drag, where the slowest animals were walking and the body of the herd drew pretty wide, which is partly why we had so many peel off at the bridge. It was bad enough to ride the drag when you herded yearlings who were relatively strong and fast, but I usually ended up there when we took the cows and calves to the range, too, and although their mothers sometimes got way ahead of them over the miles, those poor littlest calves were very tired by the fourth day and really did drag.

There wasn't a lot of cowboying to be done at that point—at least not at the back of the herd. In fact, I often got off my horse, who I knew was also tired by then, to walk alongside the calves. I could sometimes put my hand on their soft, bony little backs and not even hurry them. By the second half of the drive they didn't suddenly decide to turn and bolt from the bunch like they sometimes would when we started them up Spring Gulch Road. Instead they had resigned themselves to walking along, mile after mile, in the dust of the stronger animals, the tail end of a huge herd that strung out ahead of us for several miles. Our cattle joined with the cattle from another big ranch on the way to the range so there were thousands of animals and lots of cowboys, sometimes from two or three extended families. The cattle trailing at the back of the herd often got to be so predictable that riding with the drag was more of a social affair than it was work.

Pete always rode with the lead, so he was there to turn the herd at the place where we headed east out of Spring Gulch. And he was there when it was necessary to take them down off the road and through a gate to circumvent a cattle guard. And he was there when they needed to be funneled onto the narrow bridge to get over the Gros Ventre River and hopefully set the example for everyone coming behind them. If he and the other couple of lead riders kept the first bunch of cows on the right trail you could rely pretty well on the rest of them following. Since some of the mother cows had been part of our herd for as many as twenty years, they remembered where they were going every spring. Some of them were obviously eager to go, too, to be let loose on that fenceless range and its fresh, high-altitude green grass, which I wouldn't be surprised if they were able to think of in the abstract, and fondly.

One spring we were on the final morning of our four-day trip to the summer range with the yearlings and Pete gave me a job that elevated me, at least in my own mind, from that day forward. Somehow that morning I'd escaped the drag and had gradually ridden up through the herd until I'd gotten myself all the way to the lead bunch and was riding with Pete. We'd gathered the yearlings and started them up the road at 4:00 a.m. that day, as usual, and it was nearly noon so I was feeling pretty relaxed in the saddle. The day had warmed enough that I'd taken off my down jacket, tied it in a roll with my saddle strings, and was riding in shirtsleeves in the sun.

I wasn't pouting that morning, which I mention because I did pout from time to time when I rode with my father. Although he didn't spend much time telling me what to do in advance he wasn't opposed to hollering at me to do it faster. He never thought I was kicking my horse hard enough to get myself around a cow that had suddenly broken from the herd and he was usually right but I didn't like being yelled at in public. The horses I rode when I was little were not exactly in the same category as, say, Stinger; they weren't the kind to leap forward at the touch of your heel.

Until I got Dusty, most of my horses required a good deal of kicking before they'd break into a run, and they were often a bit overweight, and it didn't necessarily bother them to have the skinny legs of a grade-schooler flapping on their padded sides, but I don't suppose I was known for especially vigorous action myself at the time. In fact, I hated to hurry when I was little, but a waste of a half second at the beginning meant you either headed the cow off in one quick whirl or your horse and you were in for a long, hard run.

Later I learned to keep my eye on the cows and to watch their body language. I got to where I could see, before one of them bolted, if that's what she had in mind, which made heading them off in one whirl a lot more likely. But far worse than not getting quickly around a deserter was when I rode inattentively, not particularly watching my horse or the herd, and traipsed right past one, cutting it out from the bunch myself. I would kick as hard as I could then, not caring whether Pete was yelling at me or not, just hoping someone else wouldn't have to go and round up my mistake for me.

But that morning I was riding Dusty; it had been a while since Pete had yelled at me during a cattle drive, and it had been a while since I'd been mad at him. We rode along amiably, not right next to each other, each at the back of our own little bunch, but within talking distance. After some moments he said he was going to drop all the way back to Yellow-jacket Flats and check on the cattle coming behind us. He told me to go ahead and take the bunch of a hundred or so cows we were following over the next hill, on into the Dew.

I just looked at him for a second and then put my eyes on the cows and kept riding, because I wasn't certain if he'd meant what he'd said. I supposed he might actually be teasing me, and I hoped that my silence would signify either agreeing to what he'd said (if he meant it) or ignoring him (if he didn't). But without even asking for confirmation that I'd understood his instructions he turned his horse and rode off, trotting quickly away down the road.

Dusty whinnied at being left so alone and I, too, had a moment of panic. I thought all hell might break loose, that the cattle might go crazy and stampede in four directions now that the real cattleman, someone who made it look as though he controlled the herd with his mind alone, had departed. But they didn't do that. They just ambled along in the sunshine and started up the sagebrush-spotted hill in front of us. This wasn't the drag I was riding with; these were the stronger animals, and maybe they remembered coming up this trail the year before. I wonder now if I could have turned them back even if I'd wanted to.

I was all by myself then, and it seemed like the cattle ahead of me belonged to me alone and I felt all the weight of what that meant—not just the feeling of responsibility, but also of money in the bank, a connection which had been made clear to me by my mother when I was in kindergarten. I'd asked Mary to supply a recipe for the kindergarten cookbook and specified that I wanted it to be a dessert, but she said it would be better if she gave me a recipe for something with beef. "Why?" I'd asked, with all the remarkable lack of comprehension I had at the time. She answered me without commentary: "Because that's how our family makes a living."

I whistled at my bunch of cows. They were doing exactly what I needed them to do without my whistling but I couldn't help reminding myself that I was in charge. I listened for an answering whistle or holler from another cowboy but there was none. Suddenly it was a quiet morning. I could hear little but the soft thudding of hundreds of hooves into the silky dirt of the trail, nothing more than that except for the tiny squeaks of my saddle. I satisfied myself with those sounds and didn't break in with my whistle anymore.

I zigzagged my way behind them, coaxing up the stragglers on both sides, and followed the herd of cattle up the rise of the hill. When I got to the top I pulled back on the reins so I could stop and look over the wide green country spreading out below. Dusty, I think, was soaking up the same view. Not a mile ahead of us I could see the big fields of the Dew Place, with the low buildings of the old Dew homestead cradled at the bottom of the lush valley that was our destination. We were the first ones to get there, and I watched with sublime satisfaction the tail ends of a hundred Herefords kicking up gray dust as they lumbered down the bank.

10

A Fissure in the Landscape

IN THE BEST KIND OF WAY, THE DAY I TOOK THAT LEAD BUNCH OF CATTLE over the last hill before the Dew Place was the end of my childhood. It wasn't long afterwards that I was in fact out of high school, and in the years that followed I didn't herd cattle or do much in the way of other ranch work very often. I could go home when I wanted to, and sometimes I wanted to; sometimes there were even cattle drives to help with.

I was visiting the ranch once when I was in my thirties, sleeping in my old bedroom, when Mary came to awaken me at 6:00 a.m., a bit earlier than I was then in the habit of rising. "We need to get the cows off the Vogel hill," she said. The name Vogel is another artifact of a departed family, one that had once lived at what eventually became the south end of the Lower Ranch, and we always called the southernmost end of West Gros Ventre Butte the Vogel hill.

A lot of people might have mentioned the night before that they were going to ask you to get up early, so don't drink too much wine. Maybe they would've specifically said, well in advance, that your help would be needed herding cattle, and might have mentioned how long the task at hand would be expected to take, or even shared with you what its broader purpose was. But Mary simply said, standing at my bedside in the dim light of the early morning, "Hop up. We need to get the cows off the Vogel hill," and she went to put on the coffee.

My buckskin horse Dusty had died by then and I wondered who I would ride as I got into my clothes. I wondered how many head of cattle were on the hill pasture. I wondered if it would be only the two of us riding. But I just put my boots on and got myself downstairs, knowing I'd get information as I needed it—though if I'd known a bit more about the day ahead of me I might've put on some sunscreen and packed some water.

We rode with a couple of ranch hands for seven hours that day, through lunch, and it was hard riding the whole time. The cows and calves were scattered all over the butte and the calves had no idea what we were doing as we rode up on them in the trees. They were only three or four months old and had only been herded one time in their lives, when they'd been put on the hill pasture in the first place.

Coming down off the hill most of the little calves lost their mothers and quickly became an unruly mob, not knowing if they wanted to go north as we were urging them to, or south in the direction with which they were familiar. Some of the smallest ones were perfectly capable of running right under your horse's front legs, or even between the somewhat slack strands of our old barbed-wire fences if they suddenly decided to go somewhere other than what you had in mind. I wished that day that I could rope, like Brad, because it would have almost been easier to drag the little hooligans north one at a time than try to keep them gathered.

My horse and I both got a good workout that day as we ran down one wild calf after another on the rough terrain and got them back in the bunch. My mother, of course, was riding with the lead and was unable to help with the stray calves, but then, she had to stay with the lead; she was the only one who knew where we were going. It turned out we weren't simply getting the cows off the Vogel hill; we were pushing them all the way to the Bar B C, several miles to the north, which involved taking our entire herd through our neighbor Rod Lucas's pastures at the Box L where his own cows were grazing, without getting ours mixed up with his.

I was intensely grateful to discover, as we approached their property, that they knew we were coming. Apparently Mary had felt our cattle drive through their ranch was needed information on their part so there were four of the Box L cowboys out on horseback when we got there, and they helped us keep our cows going north along the fence as tight as we could so our cows didn't peel out into the Lucases' pastures and join their herd.

We did finally get the job done that day. We got the cows and calves to the Bar B C in spite of the lack of background information, but it confounded me even then whether Mary was in error for not telling me more or I was in error for not asking. And what amazed me was how little either of us had fundamentally changed. She was the same, just doing her work as always. I was the same, mostly in the dark, trying like hell to keep up.

What had changed, by then, was that Pete and Mary had gotten divorced. They were no longer partners, not in marriage and not in cattle ranching. Where my mother was concerned, of course, those two things would have to go hand in hand. I've always wondered whether Mary knew when she fell in love with my father that a New Englander like Pete would end up being the great cattleman that he turned out to be—the kind who would rescue a handful of yearlings from above Bacon Creek in December—or if she just got lucky. Knowing my mother, she didn't overanalyze it. When I was a teenager I overheard her telling a friend of hers that she'd married Pete because "he had a ski rack on the top of his car and a saddle in the back of it." When I heard Mary say that I recognized it as a remark made to get a laugh but I also thought there might be some truth to it. I knew they hadn't known each other very long before they got married.

They'd both been in their early twenties. Mary had graduated from the University of Wyoming with a history degree and then moved to Pinedale, Wyoming, to teach grade school. Pinedale is a true cowboy town on the western flank of the Wind River Mountains, surrounded by wide-open cattle and mineral country. It has a population that was, and still is, even smaller than the town of Jackson, where Mary was born and brought up. One of the best things about Pinedale from my mother's standpoint, though, was the fact that it's situated just a little more than an hour's drive from the family ranch, which she still thought of as home even when she had her own job as a schoolteacher. So she didn't exactly put down roots in Pinedale because she was up at the ranch quite a bit during the school year, as well as the whole of summer.

She got introduced to Pete in Jackson, the July after her first year of teaching, while he was wrangling dudes (the dudes may have felt they were being guided, but the cowboys referred to it as *wrangling*) and leading trail rides up into the Tetons, and she was off for the summer. Pete had been raised at a ski area in Vermont, but had followed a friend from the US Ski Team out to Wyoming to work in the off-season. My mother was an avid skier herself and had raced for the University of Wyoming, so they had that in common. Their courtship really got under way at the end of that first summer and was sustained, when they returned to their separate lives, by a letter-writing campaign the following winter.

In June of 1958, as a culmination to the winter of love letters, they were married, and Mary left her teaching job in Pinedale and moved with Pete to the California resort of Mammoth Mountain. It was at Mammoth that my father had taken his own teaching job—instructing people from Los Angeles how to make their long wooden boards turn this way and that in the elegant, floating style of 1950s skiing—and that's where they began their new life. But life at a California ski resort was not to be their real life; they weren't long into their first winter as a married couple when Wyoming and cattle ranching exerted its pull in the form of my grandfather and his real estate dealings.

Granddad had purchased another ranch about ten miles south of the Spring Gulch ranches, in an area of Jackson Hole known as South Park. I don't know if it was before or after the purchase that he decided it would be the ideal location for his daughter and new son-in-law to have their own cattle ranch, but either way Pete and Mary agreed with his assessment, recognizing a big opportunity when they saw one. So they followed Granddad's advice, left California for Wyoming, and went into debt to buy the new ranch from my grandfather. The year was 1959. My older brother, Brad, had already been born in California, but even though I was only thirteen months behind him I was born in Wyoming, as was Matt, nearly two years later.

The South Park ranch is where my parents first started using the M Lazy M on the cattle herd they were starting to build, but the misnamed brand wouldn't be in use for long. Pete and Mary's operation on the ranch in South Park was short-lived, because a few years after they started working that ranch, Granddad decided he wanted to run for governor.

That career decision ended up changing the course of Mary and Pete's lives even more than purchase of the South Park ranch had.

Granddad knew that if he did get elected it would mean relocating to Cheyenne, the state capital, 400 miles away from Jackson. In that case he'd need someone else to run the ranch, so for the second time in their relatively new marriage, he proposed a change in my parents' location.

It might not have been that enticing to my father, or even my mother, to go and run somebody else's place, but Granddad offered them the chance to buy a respectably sized piece of his property with proceeds they could get if they sold the place in South Park—or more accurately, exchanged one mortgage for another. Once again, Granddad's plan presented a good opportunity, for both sides. While the ranch in South Park had been a legitimate ranch, it was nothing compared to the land Granddad was offering them.

Granddad and his sister owned three ranches totaling nearly six thousand acres on Spring Gulch Road and they were beautiful and varied. I've already described the ranch from my own perspective as a kid but just imagine if you were looking for a place to raise cows like my parents were.

The broad Snake River ran alongside the northeast of the property and confluenced with the ropier Gros Ventre a little ways below, and then Spring Creek, wriggling with fish, flowed south the whole length of the place. The water of Spring Creek didn't freeze up in the Wyoming winters; you never had to go out and chop ice or fill tanks for cattle that did better on open fresh water anyway. There were forested mountains on both east and west, providing protected winter horse pasture; fertile hay ground in the middle, irrigated by a well-planned and executed network of ditches and canals; and river bottoms full of big cottonwoods.

Granddad wouldn't have trusted his place to many people—perhaps not to anyone more than these two. He knew my father knew horses, and that Pete, despite being an Easterner, was quickly learning cows. And I suspect he knew that in my mother's heart she'd never really left the ranch anyway.

After coming back to the ranch from the place in South Park, in fact, Mary never left home again. It seems incongruous to me now to think that she would ever have stuck with teaching school in Pinedale or selling lift tickets in California. My father, on the other hand, eventually did make his departure. I think when Mary and Pete split up it was the first time it ever occurred to me, although I was more than twenty years old, that the most fundamental facts could change—that what I thought were the immutable underpinnings of the world might not stay in their places. My parents were the two most important embodiments of the landscape and life I'd known, and when their marriage ended I really had to wonder what else might change.

I'd seen them doing ranch work side by side for more than twenty years. I'd seen them share in the toil, and the adventure, and in the fun of it, and I had no doubt that they loved each other. But it wasn't quite enough, apparently. Although over a period of time the specifics of their divorce got complicated, the one circumstance at the beginning of it—and perhaps also at the core of it—was Granddad's return from Washington.

When Granddad retired from the Senate and came back to the ranch after nearly two decades away, it was a little hard for Pete to know where he stood. Granddad wanted to be back in the cattle business in a hands-on way, but he was careful not to suddenly take control. In fact, I think he was willing to just keep things going the way his daughter and son-in-law dictated. Likewise, I think my father—although he'd run the ranch all that time, better than anyone on my mother's side of the family could've hoped for—was ready to step to the side and defer to Granddad's lead.

Despite the care exercised on both sides Granddad's return still upset the balance of things, and Pete was at loose ends. For all I know, he was also ready to finally make some independent choices about his own career. Either way, over the stretch of a few years he started shifting his focus from the ranch alone to include other things. Pete had been a pilot almost all his life, ever since the few years he had served in the air force during the Korean War. After Granddad came home Pete bought the fixed-base operation at the airport with a partner and started spending a lot more time in airplanes than he ever had before.

He was a flight instructor. He flew the air-ambulance runs out of Jackson. He flew charters to locations all over the country. He even sprayed pesticides for Teton County and had a hair-raising series of encounters with power lines. But I don't think my mother viewed any one of those variations on flying as better than the other. Even though Pete's spray plane kept the mosquitoes off us, flying airplanes could be no more than a hobby as far as Mary was concerned because for her the world turned on the ranch, and every time my father drove up Spring Gulch Road to the airport it was as if he pulled on the end of a thread which little by little unraveled the whole state of affairs.

I don't mean to say that Pete or his love for airplanes were responsible for the way my parents' marriage came apart, any more than Granddad did something wrong by returning from Washington to the ranch he'd been raised on. I understood why Pete shifted his attention to the flying business, and I understood why that adversely affected my mother. I understood why she tried to get back at him, and I understood why he one-upped her on that. I understood how all of this led to a series of choices that were hard for either one of them, in the end, to set aside. Understanding it did not make it easy, however, to sit by and watch their partnership come to an end.

I don't know all the details of how they split the assets, but I know that Pete ended up with some property north of the Bar B C, owned by my grandparents. It was not contiguous to our ranching operation or even part of it; in fact, it was almost all river bottom, as the Gros Ventre River curved right through it. It was beautiful ground, but without the dimensions or attributes of a cattle ranch. And, most significant, it was off by itself so the ranch proper would stay intact.

My father had always admired Dusty, who I still had at the time Mary and Pete split up. Living in the city I didn't have much use for him. I loved Dusty and I never forgot the way he looked the first day I saw him or the fact that I'd chosen him out of all the horses in a big herd. I hated to part with him because it meant I wouldn't own a horse (never mind that I didn't really need one). But I also hated seeing Pete leave the ranch, and I wished I could do a tiny thing to make up for it, so I told Pete he could take Dusty with him if he wanted to.

After Dusty went to live on my dad's place, according to Pete, Dusty tried to buck him off at least once a year, long past the point when they were both too old for it. Sometimes the strong-willed creature just liked to have his say, then after that he'd do as you asked, and those were both characteristics Pete seemed to admire.

Throughout my childhood my father was a bit like a movie star to me in his silk bandannas and pearl-snap shirts, riding with the lead. I admired and loved him but he was somewhat removed. Mary was the one I had to answer to on a daily basis, and she was more familiar with my shortcomings; maybe that's what put us at cross-purposes with each other from time to time. But my mother and I saw the best and worst of each other in all its detail, I think, whereas the picture I had of my father was created in broader strokes.

I looked at Pete differently after he left the ranch, however. For one thing, once neither one of us was part of the cattle operation, it meant that Pete was no longer my boss. The way I'd grown up it wasn't just that I had to obey my parents the way any kid would be expected to, but I was literally their employee, too. After I graduated from college Pete and I were pursuing completely different occupations, him in aviation, me in advertising, and our relationship changed. By then neither one of us had to worry so much about whether or not I was doing a good job.

He seemed more accessible to me then, or maybe it was just that I had more confidence in myself, but as an adult my conversations with him often provided details or context that completely changed my understanding of things that had happened years before.

After I was compelled to put my dog to sleep, for instance, I reminded Pete how he'd had to shoot our childhood pet, Pagan, and said I finally knew how hard that must have been. I let him know that I'd always understood the reason for his deception, even when I was little, and that I'd always forgiven him.

"I didn't shoot Pagan," Pete said. "We gave him away to a man we knew who lived in California, someone I was friends with from Mammoth. He was a monk, I think."

Wouldn't you know it? The one family conspiracy I'd actually been a party to, and it never existed. Oh, well. I was relieved, even four decades after the fact, to find out that Pete had not shot his dear dog.

Pete stayed a cowboy even though he was off the ranch, in that he always had horses and all that went along with that: a horse trailer, his beautiful saddle and other tack, a barn, a pasture. He often helped the few other ranchers in Jackson move and brand their cattle, or fix their fences. But he never again had cows of his own, and the closest tie he kept to the ranch afterwards, other than being our father, was that he went on fishing trips to Canada a few times with Ray Mangum. Even with the difference in their ages, they remained good friends.

My mother ran the ranch by herself for the rest of her life and she didn't stray from it, except in the way that her own father and grandfather had strayed: She ran for governor in her mid-fifties. She was a well-known Wyoming figure by then—partly because of her parents, but also because she herself had been involved in numerous statewide organizations and causes. She had some firm opinions about how the state ought to be run as opposed to how it was being run. And she'd felt, all her life, the same way her father and her father's father had—that sense of responsibility not only for the land she owned, but for the public land she used. The feeling of responsibility for that many thousands of acres, I think, was what led to a desire to have a hand in public policy. And in Wyoming there is no greater issue than the issue of land use. She didn't follow Granddad's footsteps all the way to Cheyenne, I'm afraid, because although she won the Republican primary, she wasn't able to unseat our incumbent governor at the time.

So after the campaign was over Mary went back to her ranch and her cattle. Although her father and mother lived next door, and Granddad was always involved one way or another, it was Mary who made most of the decisions. After Granddad got a hip replacement, Mary bought him a mule, which with its narrow withers was more comfortable for him than his horse was, but he didn't do that much riding. She loved having her father with her on the ranch, but it was Mary who hired and fired ranch employees, sold yearlings, and rode out through the calving mothers on frosty March mornings.

I visited her and the ranch quite often after she and Pete split up, not only when I was living in Utah, close at hand, but also during the couple of years when I was living in New York City and working for an advertising agency there. She visited me where I lived, too, quite often in Salt Lake City, and she came to New York twice while I lived there.

I loved living in New York—it was the ultimate manifestation of the desire expressed in the drawing of the one-story city that Roy Reed had penciled out for me decades earlier. And I did my best to share with Mary all the wonders of Manhattan when she visited me, but it wasn't like I was introducing her to anything that was foreign to her. During those visits she was as much a city girl as I was, hopping onto subways, hailing cabs, dancing with strangers in an Indian nightclub.

And she had her own resources, just like always, even in New York. She knew a lot of people from a lot of places around the world, partly because Jackson Hole attracted a cosmopolitan crowd, and most of those people crossed paths with my mother at some point if they stayed in Jackson long. She also traveled quite a bit by herself, more than she and my father had as a couple. She was friends with the man who owned the '21' Club, and when we went there for cocktails with him, I saw a side of the New York social scene I had not been privy to.

One evening we went to the home of one of her friends on Park Avenue for dinner. They occupied one of those apartments that had its own elevator, the doors of which, although it was situated in an elegant prewar building, opened onto a vista so white and modern you were actually startled. You had to take a moment to gather yourself before stepping out from the elevator cab.

I'd brought a boyfriend to dinner with me and he took me aside at one point, whispering that he recognized two of the art pieces in their collection from a book he owned on masterpieces of modern art. I looked around, wondering which of the ungainly sculptures or paintings in that vast apartment were masterpieces, or if they all were. Like most people in America I could recognize a Warhol, and there were more than one of those, but beyond that I was at a loss. I wished I had the education of my boyfriend, a Princeton graduate. But my mother seemed to notice the art on about the same level that she noticed the lamps and sofas. She was focused on her friends, conducting a warm and casual conversation with them on the same basis as always. They wanted to be told about the cattle business, and she obliged.

When Mary ended her visits to me—when she ended her travels and went back to Wyoming and the cattle business—she went alone. The cowboy and the ranch girl had gone their separate ways, for good. Or, more accurately, Pete went his way and my mother stayed firmly put on Spring Gulch Road. I didn't worry about my mother, running the ranch without Pete's help, the way I worried about my father having to leave after giving half his life to it.

As for their divorce, I believed I was pretty circumspect about the whole thing. I didn't blame either one of them, or blamed them both equally. At the time I didn't understand, and had no way to foresee, what all the repercussions of their split would be. So I hoped they would be happy and went on with my own life, which, as I moved from one city to another, seemed to have less and less overlap with theirs anyway.

11

Little Joe

As an adult I didn't even consider a career in the ranching business. Though I'd gotten to where I knew I was capable of making a contribution on the ranch, especially with the help of Dusty, I still didn't know if it suited me.

I'd grown to love the work, at least part of the time, and I'd gotten used to work in general. I also admired my parents for how hard they worked, and for the scope of what they took on, and I was grateful to them for raising me with jobs to do. But it was so old-fashioned, that handed-down way of life, so much the same as it had been at the turn of the twentieth century. Not only that, but it was work that didn't ever seem to pay off—at least, I didn't think it paid off financially. From what I could see about ranching, what you got, even if you succeeded very well at it, was more of it. More land and more cattle: more work.

So ranching wasn't on my list of career choices, and after I graduated from college and reneged on my enrollment in law school, I went to Salt Lake City to find a job somewhere in writing. Salt Lake was a big enough city that I had hopes of finding employment; it was within a fairly easy drive of the ranch for those times when I did want to put in an appearance; and it was also close to skiing, and those were my criteria at the time.

As for writing, I'd realized by then that it was what had gotten me through school. Although I'd taken it for granted, I could express myself on paper with some organization and clarity, and that had provided me with good grades even in subjects I didn't honestly have much affinity for, including the one I majored in, which was business administration.

Writing, whatever the subject matter, was one of the few parts of my academic life that I'd really enjoyed. And even the low-paying work of writing would be more financially rewarding than raising cows, I thought.

So for quite a while I tried to get a job in journalism, but with my lack of experience and an unrelated degree, no television station, radio station, or newspaper would hire me. Then I tried to get a job as an advertising copywriter—which according to some of my acquaintances was really scraping the bottom of the barrel—but no ad agency would have me either. Apparently the actual bottom of the barrel was somewhere underneath the ad agencies, and finally I ended up in the office of a temporary agency that placed, for the most part, secretaries. I sat there as the nice lady slowly perused the résumé I'd typed up on the electric typewriter that Mary had presented me with for my freshman year in college.

"Tractor driver," she read, crossing her legs and looking at me with a smile over her glasses. "That's so interesting."

I had an inkling that she was making an effort to be polite, and in fact, it had been suggested to me before, in the course of my trying to get jobs at various advertising agencies, that the "tractor driver" entry wasn't helping me. But I hadn't wanted to remove it, and didn't, frankly, have anything to replace it with. Besides, I thought it represented legitimate experience because it had been hard work, work I'd gotten a paycheck for.

But like everyone else I'd interviewed with, this lady had no idea how good I'd been at tractor driving or even what it entailed. As I could've told her, it wasn't just driving. It meant planning your route through sometimes complicated networks of hay so that every piece got picked up, turned over, and gathered into double rows, without wasting any trips. It involved maintaining your equipment, too, keeping your rake joints greased and your engine full of oil. Nonetheless, I felt discomfited.

"Do you think I should take that off my résumé?" I asked.

"Oh, no," she said. "I'm sure that with all your great experience you won't have any trouble finding a good job. We'll put this right in our file and give you a call."

I surmised that I hadn't ought to sit by the phone.

Finally, I did shoehorn myself into the advertising business, without the help of that lady and without the help of that résumé. I took on as many low-stakes freelance jobs as I could find, and after finally figuring out what I was doing, got hired full-time as a copywriter. But advertising was a choice so far afield of my family's experience that my mother, for one, wasn't sure for many years what it actually was that I was doing.

One day when she was visiting me in Salt Lake City we drove up alongside a city bus that had a big ad on the side of it with a headline I'd come up with on behalf of my restaurant client. As we idled by the bus I took the opportunity to explain my exciting and challenging new job to her.

"See that ad on the bus right there?" I said, pointing. "I wrote it."

Mary turned out the window and looked carefully at the side of the bus beside us, pondering, and couldn't help but respond, "It's three words."

In terms of getting sufficient credit for what I was doing, that reaction did not meet my needs, and I erroneously concluded that she thought advertising was an inconsequential pursuit. I found out later that although Mary didn't understand a whole lot about how one could be a writer in advertising, she could see that I was giving it everything I had, that no one had to tell me to "get after it." When I reached a low point in my career a number of years after the bus-board incident, I told my mother I wanted to quit because I myself didn't think I was doing anything important. Even though by that time I was creative director at the ad agency where I worked, I had the "three words" outlook on my contribution. I didn't think advertising did anything to make the world a better place, an assessment I'm sure many would agree with. But she told me I was wrong. She said there was nothing more important than doing your best at the job in front of you—that people who did that every day were the only ones who did make the world a better place.

Still, I had fallen a bit far from the tree, because no one in our family had ever gone into advertising or anything at all like it. If you strayed from ranching it was to go into the legal field or into politics, not the advertising business. Both my brothers had become lawyers, and I'd actually gone so far as to enroll in law school myself before admitting that I didn't fit that mold. Ultimately I spent twenty years writing ads and never wanted anything different than what it gave back to me. I never regretted that I didn't choose law, or didn't choose ranching. I think that in the naive part of my mind I didn't really believe I was choosing advertising in lieu of ranch life anyway.

The truth is I didn't think I had to choose, because as far as I knew the ranch would always be there for me. Whatever I happened to be doing, wherever I happened to go, however long it might take me, the ranch would still be there if and when I chose to go back. Certainly, it would still be there, stretching up to the north from our house like it had since way before I came along. It was the one everlasting feature of my life, once in the foreground, now in the background, but permanent nonetheless. Even my parents' divorce and my father's departure had not changed its boundaries.

Then one day as I toiled away my time at an advertising agency, Mary was killed in a horse accident. She died on her birthday, on the day she turned sixty-one, and when she left the world she took a lot of things with her, including the majority of my assumptions about what would or would not always be there for me. In many ways she was the last of her kind. The *New York Times* reported that at her memorial service, many people in our part of the world were not only lamenting the loss of an individual, but "the passing of an endangered human species."

Her story was known well enough by that time in her life to have her death covered by the *New York Times*, but that was not due to any degree of fame she'd achieved; she wasn't well known outside of Wyoming. It was because she represented a unique type of person and a once-venerated way of life in Jackson—a way of life that would begin to see its last days when she saw hers. Cows weren't really welcome in Jackson Hole by the time my mother died, or at least they weren't welcome on public lands. In particular, they didn't fit with the whole idea of the national park, due to the underlying fact, I suppose, that they weren't from there.

Even if people allowed that there might be some symbiotic relation-ship between grasslands and grazing animals, they wanted the grazing animals to be buffalo, not beef cattle, perhaps because buffalo are more native than cattle. I say "more" native because bison themselves are said to have originated in Eurasia, having crossed the Bering Straits at some point to get to North America. So they can also be thought of as interlopers, even though they got the jump on cattle by thousands of years.

Cattle had been brought, centuries before, from Europe and other continents, just the same as so many of the rest of us. But unlike many of us, they'd never had a say in the matter, yes or no, come or go. It was human beings who decided, and the opinion of a majority of them had changed, so cattle ranching in Jackson Hole was, by the time my mother died, already an anachronism.

I remember how surprised I was, in junior high school, when I first began to get wind of the fact that some people—people even in our own town, who'd lived there but a handful of years—did not like cattle ranching, and thought ranchers were actually destroying the West. I was surprised as hell to hear that. In my own experience we were the ones taking care of the West. My parents and grandparents took care of all the land we owned and all the land we used, and sometimes the parts in between. My mother made my brothers and me pick up other people's trash every year along approximately seven miles of Spring Gulch Road, and it would usually fill the backs of at least two pickup trucks. My great-grandfather's oft-repeated admonition to his son was, "Where you find one blade of grass, leave two."

And how tedious I thought it had been that my grandfather couldn't even walk past a piece of baling twine without picking it up and reusing it. In fact, the weight of responsibility for all that land is probably what turned me away from ranching as much as anything else did. I didn't know if I had it in me to carry the burden.

But my mother did have it in her, and if cattle ranching came to be an anachronism in Jackson Hole then perhaps my mother was one herself. She could have a chosen a different path than being a cattle rancher. She was well educated and smart, and from my own observations, I would say she had an almost unlimited tolerance for work. *Tolerance* isn't the right word, though, because I know that she loved work and thought the rest of us should too.

In any case, she never was going to choose a different path than ranching, despite the fact she might've had the opportunities, and despite the fact that in Jackson it was becoming a thing of the past. She was going to make a living in the cow business the same way her ancestors had or die trying—though as it turned out, she did both.

Having been just about born in the saddle Mary never strayed too far from it. Her forays into Laramie, Pinedale, and California might have been merely outings, in retrospect. She would always return to her leather seat and well-worn stirrups and to the ranch on Spring Gulch Road. The horse underneath it might change from time to time but the saddle would stay the same for most of her life.

She had a saddle that, between the passing of decades and the rub of her Levi's, had aged to a dark mahogany by the time she died. I thought it was beautiful, myself, but I also knew that she ultimately wanted a different saddle, because she said the best-made saddle was a Harwood. Why she hadn't bought herself a Harwood years earlier I do not know, because Pete had one. But my mother had a saddle she was comfortable in, and I think in her mind she was never too far from it, never too far from the back of a horse or the shifting margins of a cattle herd.

She got up early that day. Since it was her birthday she could have chosen to sleep in, to be treated to a restaurant breakfast, or to have taken herself off to one of Jackson's several spas to enjoy what would have been the first pedicure of her life. But she chose work, and it happened that the work which needed to be done that day was her favorite kind: herding cattle. She was in the process of moving them mostly north and a little east, toward their summer feeding grounds, which were at that time thirty miles from their home pastures.

By then we'd sold our grazing permit on Bacon Creek and the cattle drive was no longer up the Gros Ventre River. Our family had finally decided in the 1980s that the four-day drive was too far, there was too much shrink on the cattle, and there were too many bears in the backcountry. Instead, they trailed up through Mormon Row to a part of Grand Teton National Park known as the Elk Ranch, over ground that had once been privately owned cattle ranches, hand-hewn places tiled up alongside the old road named for the religious preferences of its early settlers.

The Mormon Row ranch steads are all now uninhabited, and also part of Grand Teton National Park. Since our family had been grazing cattle on parkland since before the national park had been established, we had some historical justification, and my mother had been able to retain the ranch's grazing permit. Congress had made the term of the permit her own lifetime, however, because as I said, most people in our country, and more and more of them in our own county, wanted cows out of the park as soon as possible, if not off all public lands.

The lifetime term of the grazing permit didn't worry any of us, though. Mary had descended from rugged stock, and I'm sure she assumed she'd get another twenty or even thirty years' use out of the permit before my brothers and I, as her progeny, would have to petition Congress in a long-shot bid for an extension.

That morning, Mary was riding with her husband of less than a year, Richard Steinhour. She'd remained single for a decade and a half following her divorce from Pete, but after all that time she'd found someone she clicked with, and Richard was willing to leave his home and his life in urban Colorado to move onto the ranch and into her life, her business, and her bevy of friends. You pretty much had to come to her, and he was apparently willing to.

Though Mary hadn't succeeded in her run for governor, in the course of attempting it she'd met Richard. He'd sent her a campaign contribution, and she'd sent him a thank-you note; then he wrote her a letter, and so on. As I said, they'd been married only a matter of months before she died. I never knew Richard that well and he is also dead now. I had quickly grown to appreciate, and then to love, my father's wife Leslie (who he'd married a decade earlier), but I didn't know Richard long enough. He seemed to be very kind—a gentleman. I don't believe he was the type who would have attempted or survived a December ride through a blizzard all the way to the Dew Place to drag four yearlings across the ice of Heifer Creek. But I wouldn't meet that standard myself, and I didn't fault my mother for wanting companionship, or for wanting a different kind than what she'd had before.

Mary and Richard arrived at the back of the herd, which they'd already moved about a third of the way to their destination the day before, and got their saddled horses out of the trailer at about 7:30 that morning.

It was June 21, and by the look of it, that day epitomized the summer solstice: a few bunchy clouds sitting placidly in a saturated blue sky, that spot in northwest Wyoming having finally tilted close enough to the sun that some of its warmth could actually soak into the ground and the new grass, the cattle, and the riders. The Wyoming winter had been long and recalcitrant, as always, but had finally started to give way sometime in early May and on June 21, it was at long last summer.

My mother was riding a horse she called Little Joe. He was a pretty thing, a medium sorrel color with a smallish head, and for some reason, Mary had let his mane and tail get a bit longer than she usually preferred. He was also, unlike any other horse I can remember her having, a little spoiled. I'd ridden him the summer before and found that he was choosy about certain things, such as water crossings. He reared up with me when I insisted he wade through shallow East Miner Creek up at the Bar Double R. Mary wasn't the type of person to ever abuse her horses but she wasn't one to let them misbehave, either. I think Little Joe was spoiled before he came into my mother's possession.

The cattle knew where they were going that morning, and it was easy riding for a few hours. Little Joe was interested enough in cattle and had become a pretty good cow horse under the steadfast tutelage of my mother. Richard's horse was a bit green but so was Richard and that didn't matter. There was nothing tricky about pushing the herd up the road and across the gentle, open pastures of Mormon Row. It was no problem for just the two cowboys to keep a handle on things even though there were a thousand head of cows and calves trailing out in front of them.

But then a little thing—one that should have been inconsequential, or at least easy enough to ride around—managed to get in their way. There was a small piece of the pasture, about halfway between the Mormon Row road and the eastern slopes of Blacktail Butte, a quarter-mile to its west, that had been fenced in by the Park Service so their range management people could keep track of the difference between grass that had been affected by the passing herd and grass that remained untouched inside the fence. When my mother rode Little Joe past this innocuous barricade, he determined that he didn't like it, and jumped sideways.

In my mind since then I've liked to try and envision a different out-come to this little incident, a version of events in which my mother just clucked at her horse and kept on going, turning Little Joe north in the sunshine with the herd of cattle as they made their way to another tranquil summer of green grass on their resplendent open range. In other words, a version of events in which she did what I probably would have done, just as I'd kept going in similar circumstances a few decades earlier. My horse had jumped sideways from a bloat-dead cow on the side of the trail not far from where my mother was riding that day, and I just kept on going and didn't look back.

But Mary would never have permitted Little Joe to do that—to proceed under the impression that it was acceptable to her, a working cowboy, that he had behaved so foolishly. Even though he'd caused no harm on that occasion, maybe the next time he jumped away from a harmless stationary object he would be ferrying a less-experienced rider, or maybe he'd be on slippery ground, or maybe he'd be in the middle of serious business at the heels of a renegade cow.

So my mother set out to instruct Little Joe that he had nothing to fear from the fence, that he was capable of walking by it without lurching away, and that she was going to insist he did so. She turned back and made him take another look at it. But once again he lunged sideways with her, acting even more terrorized by the orange barricade. So once again she turned him back, and rode past it a third time. On that third pass Little Joe reared up suddenly and even more forcefully than he himself must have intended. He hurled himself completely over backwards, so quickly that my mother didn't have time to throw herself in one direction or the other to get out of the way of this thousand-pound animal, falling, falling down fast to ground that did not yield.

Richard had been watching my mother take her horse through this repetitive exercise and he saw her go down, but he was surprised to see, after Little Joe righted himself and scrambled up from the dirt, that Mary did not. Richard came out of his stirrups and ran to her, letting both his horse and hers wander off, the reins of their bridles dragging the ground. He spoke to her as she lay there, flat on her back. He asked her if she was all right, knowing that if there was an affirmative answer she'd be up, that probably she'd be swinging a leg over the seat of her saddle by then. She looked at him but could not speak. She only picked up her right hand for a moment, gesturing, he thought, to Little Joe, and that was the last move she made.

Richard ran for the highway.

My response to the phone call I got from Brad and my sister-in-law that morning, as far as I can remember, is that I made no meaningful utterance. This news clutched me as if I'd plunged into the early spring waters of the Gros Ventre River again; my lungs seized up and my voice froze down in my throat. I don't remember much of what Brad said to me either, except for "Come home."

Then I unfroze. I cried the entire flight between Salt Lake City and Jackson Hole. I couldn't believe that my mother had been killed in such a way. On horseback was about the last way I'd have expected her life to end, and I was crying from incredulity as well as grief. As I sat there on the airplane with my shoulders shaking, I didn't care who saw me or how uncomfortable I was making them. *Please,* I thought, *just let them feel miserable, too.* I threw myself into my grandmother's arms and bawled on her shoulder as soon as I got to the ranch. I cried to my grandfather and to my father, and to both of my brothers, and to my dog. I cried to everyone who called me on the phone, and I cried myself to sleep that night, back in my old bed.

As I sobbed into my pillow, much as I tried to ignore it, I couldn't help but listen to the cacophony of the violent summer storm that had gathered itself up and then detonated, hard, over our valley that night. The rainfall was so heavy and the thunder so frequent, so earsplitting, that I imagined if I ventured beyond the front door I would immediately be struck by lightning. I pulled the pillow down on my head and just wished I could cry without listening to it. I wanted to concentrate on my misery without that deafening distraction, and I resented the rainstorm for going about its business as though the Earth had suffered no calamity. After that, when someone wrote in a letter to my grandparents that the spectacular storm was Mary's welcome into heaven, I remembered with bitterness how the storm had irritated rather than awed me, and wondered if maybe the rainstorm had known of a calamity after all.

Later Brad told me how he and Granddad were led into a little room at the hospital shortly after Mary had arrived in the ambulance. They were allowed to look at her, to lift the sheet and to see for themselves that she'd died with her boots on. I felt some pride when this scene was described to me that she had died in her cowboy boots. That she had died working. This was the first bit of salve to my injured feelings. For some reason it makes you feel better instead of worse, when you've lost someone, to hear from others what a great person your loved one was, and for me the fact that my mother died in her cowboy boots amounted to that.

A meaningful tribute was also paid to her at the memorial service that was held in town a few days later, when a cowboy named Bob Lucas got up from where he sat in the pew and strode to the church piano. I didn't know how that had been arranged and I wasn't expecting it.

Bob was the son of Rod and Joyce Lucas, one of the few other ranching families on Spring Gulch Road, and he'd been raised on their ranch, the Box L. He was about ten years older than I was so I didn't know him that well before I left town, but I visited the ranch often, and I did get to know him well after I'd moved away because he was a close friend to both my mother and father, not just before they split up but afterwards, too. His family had been around the cow business and that part of Wyoming as long as ours had, and he was an accomplished horse trainer and a cowboy to his marrow.

My mother loved him, in fact, in the way you can love someone out of sheer admiration. Although he was talented and intelligent, and also handsome, he was almost impossibly modest, and for that reason as much as any other he was the kind of person my mother held in high esteem.

Bob Lucas was a surprising person, too; apparently he'd been taking piano lessons for some time. He had his cowboy hat off in church that day and his forehead floated pale above his deep-set eyes and tanned cheeks as he moved his calloused fingers skillfully over the keys, drawing from them a heartbreakingly beautiful song.

My brothers and I didn't speak publicly that day, but we were each asked to share a few stories and favorite memories about Mary for the eulogist to recount, and Matt asked the speaker to pass on what became an iconic story. Along with Bob Lucas playing the piano, it's what I remember most clearly about her memorial service, with all the things that were said, with all the accomplishments that were mentioned, with all the fog of the sadness I was wandering in.

It was a story of the instructions Mary had given Matt when she'd asked him to take control of the ranch during her gubernatorial campaign. She'd won the Republican primary without turning her life upside down, but she knew her campaign for the general election would take her off the ranch for several months. Mary found herself in the same position her father had been in thirty years before: She needed someone to set aside what they were doing, and to come back to the ranch and take over—at least for the length of the campaign, but if things went well, then possibly for many years.

Brad and Kate were living in Arizona at that time, both at the start of their law careers. I had just moved from New York to Utah, and was working long hours at an advertising agency. But Matt, except when he was getting his undergraduate degree, had never left Wyoming.

At that time he was the Assistant County Attorney in Campbell County, living in the county seat of Gillette. Gillette bills itself as the "Energy Capital of the Nation" because of the fact that Campbell County produces over 30 percent of the nation's coal for electricity, in addition to vast reserves of oil and natural gas. The flow of the occasionally rowdy mine workers and oilfield roughnecks in and out of Gillette had made the prosecutor's office an interesting place to be, but it wasn't a job Matt wanted to do forever. So he agreed to it when Mary asked him to come and manage the ranch operation while she was canvassing the state.

There could hardly have been more at stake for my mother when she handed control of the 2,000-cow operation to her youngest son. But as I've said, she was never big on giving out instructions, and even in the case of handing her whole ranch over she was short on advice. As Matt told the story, she had but one suggestion: "When you're gathering up the cows," she said, "you've got to ride the very outside fence line. You'll ride harder and take longer than anyone else, but it's the only way to make sure you're not leaving a single animal behind."

With that, she left for Cheyenne. Matt figured out how to run the ranch, and did it his own way, as Mary wanted him to.

It was the same advice, so scant and yet so very vast, that she'd given all three of us, not in those words but by the way we were raised. Don't go easy on yourself, be the last one home, and everything else will come to you.

In the days that followed her memorial service it was "Ride the outside fence line" that stuck with me—a way to remember how Mary had lived her life and wanted me to live mine.

A Slow Dissolve

A FEW DAYS AFTER THE SERVICE MY BROTHERS AND I, RICHARD, MY FATHER, Bob Lucas, and some friends who were good riders trailered our horses up to Mormon Row at four o'clock in the morning.

Granddad had explained to me, when I was small and complaining to him about the middle-of-the-night cowboying my parents made us do, that when you herd cattle, it's best to start early and quit about lunchtime, especially if you're moving cows and calves. If the calves are just waking up and haven't had a chance to start suckling yet, they'll be a lot more interested in keeping up with their mothers.

So we arrived at Mormon Row hours before the sun was up. The cattle had been left to mill around for several days halfway between the ranch and their summer range while we attended to Mary's memorial service and the people who came to bid her good-bye, and they seemed glad to see us. But they were scattered pretty wide and we were grateful that we had plenty of help to get them gathered up and started, once again, north.

I rode in the worn comfort of my mother's old saddle that morning, and I figured from that day forward it would be my saddle. By then I no longer had one of my own. The saddle I'd used in high school was a hand-me-down, and it had been handed along when I moved out, becoming part of the general inventory on the ranch, used by anyone who needed to borrow tack.

I didn't own a horse, either. Dusty had died of old age several years before, and Pete—in what I thought was an uncharacteristically sentimental gesture, and one that I was extremely grateful for—had dug him a grave with the backhoe on his place north of the Bar B C.

Bob Lucas came to my rescue that day. Knowing I wouldn't want to take Little Joe out on the cattle drive, he provided me with a sweet gray horse to ride. Although I'm sure my mother would not have wanted us to put the blame on Little Joe, he wasn't going to be of any use to us. He'd been caught up at Mormon Row by someone the afternoon of Mary's death, hauled in a trailer back to Spring Gulch, and put out to graze by himself in one of the horse pastures at the Lower Ranch. Later Bob came by with his own horse trailer, loaded up Little Joe, and took him away to I don't know where. I never saw him again. Bob took it upon himself to leave a well-behaved sorrel by the name of Tim in Little Joe's place, and, as far as he was concerned, when he dropped Tim off at our place that was the end of the transaction.

I rode steeped in self-pity all day, not making an effort at conversation with the other cowboys when I came alongside them. I felt I would be justified in dismounting from Bob's horse and throwing myself on the ground. I tried to appreciate the good nature of the gray horse Bob had provided me with, and I tried to succumb to the thrill of the swift run we had going north across the sagebrush of Antelope Flats, still in darkness. And most of all, I tried to be thankful for the rarest opportunity I'd had in a span of many years, which was riding behind cattle with Brad, Matt, and Pete again. But my mother's absence at the outskirts of the herd was palpable.

A week or so after we finished the cattle drive, my brothers and I met with the attorney who'd helped our family for many years with estate planning, something I'd always known my parents and grandparents were concerned with like most people in agriculture. Federal inheritance taxes of 55 percent usually make it impossible to pass a large piece of land on to your children. Often, the only way inheritance taxes can be paid is for the land to be sold—or at least, for half of the land to be sold—which in many cases makes the operation unworkable. So you try to figure out ways to circumvent the tax, including giving the land away to your heirs during your lifetime. That method had made up the bulk of my grandparents' estate plan, and they'd been giving land to my mother for many years, as fast as the law allowed. The plan backfired when, to everyone's surprise, her death preceded theirs. By that time she owned the entire Bar B C.

Our attorney was plain with us about what that meant. "You realize," he said as Brad and Matt and I gazed across the desk at him in his office in Idaho Falls, still a bit stunned, "that you're going to have to sell your mother's ranch." I'm sure that pronouncement was particularly hard on Brad, because by then he and Kate had left Arizona, moved their law practice to Jackson, and were installed on Spring Gulch Road with their two young boys. They lived on the Lower Ranch, not the Bar B C, but any change in our operation's boundaries would have a material effect on them, and perhaps a bigger emotional impact than it would have on me or Matt, because it would happen right in front of them.

Our attorney explained our situation partly by giving us a daunting estimate of how much we might owe in inheritance taxes. But according to him, that wasn't even the most serious issue. He described to us how, inheritance taxes aside, it would be very hard on the three of us to jointly own a piece of property, even one as large as the Bar B C. From a practical standpoint only one family could probably reside there. And he told us that, even if we were for some reason willing to own it jointly, it was unreasonable to expect our own children, however many of them there might someday be, to own it jointly. It was not a sustainable formula.

There was an old ranch to the west of us that had been handed down through the various generations to the point where it was owned by more than a dozen heirs. Apparently they'd had the ability to pay whatever estate taxes there'd been, but none of them had ever been able to buy the others out, and with so many owners they were, for all intents and purposes, immobilized. Most of them didn't even live in Wyoming, and some of them were aging and more than ready to collect their inheritance, but it was nearly impossible to agree on a course of action.

I don't know how clear-eyed Brad and Matt were during that meeting, but as for myself, I wasn't ready to recognize the lawyer's logic. Despite the fact that all my life I took the ranch and everything it represented for granted; despite the fact that half the time growing up I didn't even think I fit in there, and had found that I did fit in elsewhere; despite the fact that I'd left it behind many years before and didn't miss it, as far as I knew—I didn't like the prospect of losing it, and in my mind I took up what I thought was a valiant position.

I silently vowed that we would not sell. I assured myself during that meeting with the lawyer that the ranch and all that it meant, everything my ancestors had built and my mother and father had worked so hard to improve and preserve, would not be carved apart by her unexpected death. We'd hold it together, we'd continue on just as she would have. Hadn't we been out herding cattle within a week of her demise?

But I didn't say any of those things during that meeting, or even afterwards—not to the attorney, or to either of my brothers. I'm afraid I suspected as soon as I formulated those thoughts that they didn't hold much water. You could divide up money, but there was no way of fairly dividing up the Bar B C; it wasn't just a flat piece of unvarying ground, a chessboard where this square was as good as that one. It had a forested river bottom on this part and a stream along that one, mostly hay meadows down the center, but also mountains on the east and west, which were beautiful and valuable (although, as far as agriculture went, relatively unproductive). Who would get what was a question that couldn't be answered equitably.

And with the death of my mother, there was no grazing permit, nowhere for the cows to go in the summer so we could grow hay to feed them in the winter. Grazing on public lands had been an essential part of the operation. No one could own enough private land in Jackson Hole to make a productive cattle ranch work any other way—not in a county where 97 percent of the ground was held by the government. And it seemed that very few people would be sad to see our cows go.

So the era of building was about to give way to the era of dissolution. My generation would be the one to take it apart. My great-grandfather and great-grandmother, P.C. and Sylvia, had patched the ranch together, gotten it fenced, dug the irrigation ditches, and bought the first cows. My great-aunts and -uncles, my parents and grandparents, and more than one generation of ranch hands had given their lives to it. Granddad had described to me how he and his siblings, as children, had uprooted the sagebrush with their mother and father by dragging a piece of railroad rail attached to a heavy log over all those acres of ground. Granddad's older sisters had stacked the uprooted brush and set fire to it, one stubborn pile at a time. By the time I came along you would've thought the pastures had never been anything but lovely grass, and for my generation, they weren't.

My brothers and I were very slow to face all the tasks and transactions, the fallout of Mary's death. We didn't even get her personal belongings sorted out for nearly two years, and by then I was surprised at how few of them seemed to mean anything. I did come upon mementos she'd kept of Brad, Matt, and me in the top drawer of her bathroom vanity. The three items seemed somewhat randomly selected, but apparently had represented something to my mother, and she'd kept them alongside her hairbrush and hand lotion where she would see them every day.

One was a receipt from a jewelry store in New York but there were no purchases itemized there, just the scrawled lettering of Brad's very young hand, reading "Lobe you Mary." And there was a recipe that had been written by Matt for a kindergarten cookbook, for which they'd asked the students to provide instructions for the best thing their mom cooked for them. Matt had said about shrimp that you "cook until nighttime." As for me, there was a book of poetry I'd written in grade school, full of laborious rhymes and rather crudely bound together with staples, but I remembered the time I'd taken with it and that I'd given it to my mother.

Later I was going through the closets in her back hall, not necessarily opening all of the containers, but the dated look of one particular box drew my attention. It had a decorative lid and looked as if it might've contained a woolen scarf from a 1950s department store. When I opened the box I found not a scarf but all my parents' love letters, aged but intact, tucked in their envelopes.

Mary had saved all of their correspondence from the winter of 1957–58, perhaps twenty letters in all, resting in that box for forty years. I took them from their envelopes in chronological order according to the postmarks and read them all as I sat there on the floor of the hallway next to her storage cabinets. That I was invading Mary and Pete's privacy didn't seem relevant at the time, because the letters revealed a world that, after a series of events—including my leaving home, my parents splitting up, both of them getting remarried, and then my mother dying—no longer existed. So I helped myself to each tender word and then I put the letters back in the box, and I took them with me when I left her house that day without mentioning their existence to either of my brothers. I wanted the letters and the evidence that there'd been more to their partnership from the beginning than a saddle and a ski rack.

The other items we split up as fairly as we could, and finally, eight years after Mary died, we came to terms with the inevitable and sold the Bar B C.

Despite the fact that it took eight years, and that I didn't admit it to myself at the time, I think we all knew as we left our attorney's office that afternoon in June 1996, that it was over. That the ranch we knew and the life it had provided for us had come to an end, and it had ended, as I found out later, while my mother was on the waiting list for a Harwood.

Back to the Pig Farm, and to Mormon Row

VERY LITTLE COULD BE PRETTIER THAN WHAT YOU SEE FROM THE PIG Farm on an Indian summer day when the grain across the road is ready for harvesting. Looking south across the dirt lane to the Wilsons', if our big M Lazy M sign isn't in your way, you can take in what seems like all the wide sky of Wyoming, and rolling underneath it, the undulating land of the Wilsons' barley fields. The clouds typically lumber up in shades of gray from the southwest, gathering in the warm wind running from over by the south end of the Big Hole Mountains in Idaho, that other state to the west. As you look across the barbed-wire fence you can see the wind coming for you across the silken tassels of barley beards, wave after rif-fling golden wave. The ripe barley in the wind is like fire, the way it lashes quickly along without going anywhere, the way it holds your eye. You can sit and watch this scene for hours: the storm clouds collecting themselves, the gentle rise and fall of the barley sea, the Idahoan wind coming to push at your hat.

The view is as beautiful as always, in other words, and the rest of it's still a struggle. A struggle against the weather, a struggle against the short growing season, and a struggle against my own shortcomings as a farmer.

I finally had the fields sprayed with a broadleaf poison to kill the alfalfa once and for all. Before that we had plowed up the old crops, twice, and reseeded the entire acreage with a mix of orchard grass, fescue, and brome, twice. The first time we got the seed in late because constant early rains turned the plowed fields to mud and the seeders couldn't drive their vehicles out on the fields without getting mired in the muck. Then once we got the seed down the weather went the opposite way, turning dry and windy for the rest of the summer. We tried to keep the fields irrigated, but I think half the seed blew away, and the hardy old alfalfa plants were eager to volunteer in place of the precious new pasture grass.

The second spring I went to the Pig Farm and harrowed the ground myself the day after Simplot's crew got the new seed in. (A harrow is an implement with numerous downward-pointing spikes that stir up the surface of the dirt without digging too far under, and, when dragged behind your tractor, works like a rake to cover over and mix in the seed.) I still didn't know a lot about farming but I was learning what not to do, at least, and I wanted to push that dear seed into the dirt in person. I wasn't going to let it sit on the surface and maybe dry out and maybe blow away. I wanted every kernel to latch on to the ground and grow.

I had to borrow a tractor from Brad to pull the harrow. It was a Czechoslovakian job and underpowered for all the drag of the twenty-four-foot harrow, which I'd had to rent from an Alta neighbor. I wouldn't have any of my own equipment until later that summer, when I mentioned to Brad that I was looking for an old Farmall Super C, in case he knew anybody who had one to sell. I was hoping to find the exact same kind of tractor I'd driven in high school, I told him, for sentimental as well as practical reasons. I assumed the operation of the thing would all come back to me once I had a short refresher course, and I remembered how simple this model of tractor was (for me) to maintain and (for my father) to fix.

Brad said I didn't have to look for a Super C, though. He said I could have the one still sitting in the equipment shed behind the old shop—the one I'd probably put five thousand miles on just going up and down the hayfields at the Lower Ranch all those years. It was parked right underneath the place where we'd built the elaborate fort in the rafters. Later in the summer my husband Michael, Brad, and a friend of Brad's spent the morning getting the Super C running and brought it over Teton Pass to the Pig Farm. The only part they'd had to replace was the battery; the rest of the tractor's resurrection was just a matter of changing fluids, cleaning the spark plugs, and filling the gas tank. The sound of the engine on the fifty-six-year-old Farmall was enough to make me laugh out loud the first time I pulled the starter, it was so friendly to me.

But for harrowing the fields at the Pig Farm that day it was the Czech machine I had the use of. I came out of the pig barn on a very cold April morning to see the tractor sitting there waiting, along with the harrow. Pete had taken his flatbed trailer over to the Lower Ranch and brought the tractor back to the Pig Farm for me. It was a big favor on my father's part, but Pete was in the habit by then of helping Brad and Matt on their places, and he seemed just as glad to help me with mine, only four miles down the road from his. Our neighbor to the south, Lorin Wilson, the one with the beautiful barley fields, had arranged for me to rent the harrow from his dad, and Lorin had also taken the trouble to deliver it to the Pig Farm. So between my brother, my dad, and my neighbor, all I had to do was hitch up and go.

I climbed up into the seat of Brad's tractor and laughed to myself. For padding on the stiff metal seat there was a folded pair of old work coveralls—typical, I thought, of the Lower Ranch machinery, and just about as I remembered it. But never mind; I sat myself down on the folded clothing and started up the motor.

The Czech tractor was a simple thing to operate, not too big, and probably would have been ideal for pulling a rake over on the Lower Ranch, where the ground was flat for miles. But on the hilly ground of the Pig Farm, I struggled with it. It was only two-wheel drive, and as I headed up the slopes of our up-down, up-down fields with the wide harrow behind me, the tractor's back wheels would start to spin and dig in.

I reminded myself of Ray, dragging the ditcher across the hayfields with the old diesel Cat forty years before. I didn't really like digging trenches on our hillsides with the spinning tires, and even more than that, I didn't like the idea of flipping over backwards and killing myself. I still remembered nearly flipping the Super C when I was in junior high by putting it in fourth gear and popping the clutch, so I knew how easy it was to do.

The front end of the Czech tractor felt uncomfortably light as I made my uneasy way up our hillsides, the harrow hitched by a chain and not a rigid tongue. Neither the chain nor the harrow would have been any impediment to my backwards flip the way the big side-delivery rake had been thirty years before. A couple of times I realized I wasn't going to make it, which meant turning the whole contraption, tractor and harrow both, 180 degrees on the side of the hill, which was nearly as hard on the poor little tractor as continuing up would have been. Finally I decided I'd have to harrow the hillsides driving sideways, although that didn't feel much safer.

Lorin was to the south of our place doing his own plowing that day and apparently he was watching me as I wrestled the harrow against gravity. (As I said, the harrow belonged to his father.) I guess Lorin and his family had been surprised and grateful when the Pig Farm was sold to someone who wanted to keep it in agriculture, and the Wilsons, along with most of our other Alta neighbors, actually welcome cows. So although I didn't know Lorin that well at the time, he kept insisting on trying to help me. In fact, he'd offered to lend me his own tractor for the harrowing, as well as arranging for the harrow, but I'd turned him down. I said I already had a tractor coming over from the Spring Gulch ranch and that I was all taken care of, thank you. So I toiled slowly through forty acres the first day, and on top of my slow progress and my scuffles with the wrinkled nature of the Pig Farm pastures, I nearly froze myself in the frigid Wyoming spring.

The next morning before I got started Lorin showed up very early with a shiny blue New Holland tractor. It only had a few hours on it, four-wheel drive, and an electronic transmission with twelve gears: torque galore. By then I was ready to accept his generosity. By then I'd discovered there was a note of encouragement from Lorin tucked into the pair of coveralls that had padded the seat of the Czechoslovakian tractor, that in fact they were Lorin's own coveralls and he'd folded them up and left them right there on the tractor seat for me, knowing I wouldn't be warm enough in whatever I'd brought from Salt Lake City. I'd just sat on those nice lined coveralls and his note all day, for nine hours and forty acres with frost accumulating on my jeans.

With Lorin's tractor I harrowed the remaining eighty acres in the same amount of time it had taken me to do forty the day before, and furthermore I never felt that my life was in danger. I did my best to let it all come back to me—how good I'd supposedly been at tractor driving—rotating the harrow as I turned at the end of each row within a few feet of our new fence posts. It was sunnier that second day, too, and I was dogged by red-tailed hawks in the blue skies all day, sometimes four of them at a time. It made me feel welcome on the place to have their company. They watched me stir up the rodents as I went and I felt certain they were showing off. One of them would wheel in for a catch with more flourish than was certainly necessary. One of them would stand rigid not twenty feet from me as a vole struggled in its beak, indifferent to the best hawk screeches I could come up with as I went by.

Of course, my adventure with the harrow is just another measure of how different the Pig Farm is from the ranches in Spring Gulch. Over on the other side the fields never needed harrowing—not just because they didn't need seeding, but because they didn't even need to be smoothed out every year as the Pig Farm pastures do. At first, I couldn't understand how our Pig Farm fields got so rough, how they got so dug up by gophers. I never remembered the Lower Ranch or the Bar B C being riddled with gopher holes the way the Pig Farm pastures are. I finally asked Lorin Wilson about it.

"I wonder why we have so many gophers over here," I remarked one day, adding, "We never had all these gopher holes and mounds over in Jackson."

He looked at me with a slight smile. "Well," he said, in his slow and patient country voice, "didn't you do flood irrigation over there?"

It was almost like I'd just had the difference between up and down explained to me by my mother. Of course, the fields of the Spring Gulch ranches east of the Tetons were level, and divided into sections by irrigation ditches, which Ray or Roy would dam to let the water evenly flow over the fields, at the same time flooding the gopher holes.

And our fields over on the east side of the Tetons were not only level, but also populated with native grasses that came back thick every year with just an application of ditch water and the fertilization they got from being occupied by cattle. There wasn't any farming. There wasn't any seeding or harrowing, at least not for my generation. All we gave it was a couple of passes in the spring with a homemade brush-drag to break up the big pieces of manure.

But the Pig Farm has provided us with some good work to do, and I've been recording the pertinent episodes in the Pig Farm journal in the style of my ancestors: "84 tons baled on N.W. 40," or "Moved cows to east pasture." (Pete eventually shared with me his own journal entry from the day I was born: "Mary went to the hospital, had a baby girl, we branded 400 head of calves.") Some of the steadiest work is irrigating, and Lorin's teenage boys have taught Belle and Joe how to move the pipe and operate the industrial-size sprinkler systems. So my children are now, unbeknownst to them, following in the footsteps of the matchless Ray Mangum in that they're our full-time irrigators.

And it feels good to look out across the fields now where I can see their work paying off. Where I can see, on the still-unfamiliar contours of our up-down land, a familiar texture. One that's not fluffy but velvety. It's grass. And we're trying again to pasture cattle on it, now that the alfalfa seems to be finally done away with, and so far we haven't lost any more animals.

I do still wonder sometimes why I'm so hell-bent on having cows, especially when we're only at the Pig Farm during the summer and have to ship them back and forth. It's hard to explain to people, even to your own husband and children, what cows can add to your life if you haven't lived around them. I've told Michael about the way I used to sing at the hayloft window and draw the cows into the corral to listen to me, one by one. To him this is a funny story and it might even endear him to cows, but I know it doesn't convey the satisfaction of living with cattle, of living alongside pastures milling with your own herd. When you can look out from your home in the evening and see your cattle in the dimming distance with their heads down in the grass, you think to yourself, "Doing fine," and the sense of stewardship, as I finally came to realize, lifts you rather than burdens you.

Mary showed me once that if you go out into a cow pasture and lie on your back and hold still and be quiet, you'll find that often the cows will eventually wander up to you. One by one they'll gather around you and, if you don't move, they'll start to sniff you and maybe even taste you with their long, slippery tongues. At least, that's how the cows on our ranch behaved, but I think I've already mentioned that we were gentle with them.

I think my mother felt like a mother to them all. She and my father, even with a thousand head of mother cows, knew one cow from the other. Mary was one of the first people I knew to buy a personal computer—she purchased one as soon as they were available back in the 1980s—and eventually created a database of all the mother cows who were the foundation of the herd: when they were born, when they were vaccinated, when they had their calves, whether they had trouble birthing. She saw them through all the events of their lives, some of them for decades, and kept track of their histories.

It's some of their descendants that we now pasture at the Pig Farm in the summertime. They'll never go out on the open range. They're confined to the tight margins of our modest acreage, but they're easy to see from the house and I give them the best care I can and at least they'll never have to be dragged over Heifer Creek in the middle of winter.

I even found a horse to buy. Pete and I had talked a few times, as I contemplated different horses, about the kind of horse Dusty was, how smart, how willful. I reminded him during a phone call about how he'd actually gone out of his way to dig a grave for Dusty rather than putting him in the bone pile, which as I said earlier I thought was "uncharacteristically sentimental." But the things I didn't know were still in plentiful supply.

"Maybe I didn't show my emotions," Pete said, "but I dug a grave for Perk." And his voice faltered over the phone as he continued with the names of some of his most loved horses. "And also Tony. And Skippy."

Thinking of Dusty, I drove by the horse ranch in Ashton, Idaho, where Mary and I had picked him up more than thirty years ago, but they must've gone out of business. Either that or died off, because as I remember the horse breeder was not a young man the day my mom and I bought horses there. I felt a little foolish as I slowed down on the highway, looking out across the fields as if I expected to see a buckskin colt running by when there was only a potato combine rolling along, stirring up its own plume of dust.

Much later I found a ten-year-old gelding being sold by one of the best trainers in the Teton Valley, and I brought him home. I named him Paddy, because of the beautiful red color of his sorrel coat, and so far we get along pretty well, in spite of the fact that he's sometimes a little too independent-minded. And willful.

I bought myself a new saddle, too, because I didn't end up with my mother's saddle after all. (My saddle's not a Harwood, but it was made by Stacy Jensen, who used to work for Dale Harwood.) It had been suggested that we give Mary's saddle to her alma mater, the University of Wyoming, and it now rests in a glass case in Laramie. Though she loved the University it seems incongruous, to me, that it sits there. Partly because I would have liked to own it myself, and partly because it doesn't really seem like her, the glass case.

As for Mary's jeans, shirt, and fleece top, I still have them in the box Kathy sent them in. I've never asked her why she sent them to me or if she was going to do so why she chose to wait fourteen years. I can imagine myself in her position, though; the clothes really weren't hers to throw away, but she might've worried it would be too hurtful to send them to one of Mary's children. I can imagine how I would have dithered, myself, for fourteen years.

Besides the new horse and saddle I indulged myself in a tepee. My views on old buildings versus new had changed 180 degrees by the time we bought the Pig Farm, and we'd gone to some trouble to save a dozen of the old pigsties, as well as the cinder-block farrowing barn where all the piglets were born, and a small log granary. I was at home with the old structures, decrepit as some of them were. But a tepee would literally round things out, I felt, giving silent thanks to Roy Reed Martin and how much his pursuit of "the Indian way" had added to the adventure that was my upbringing.

It took some trouble for four of us—Pete, my stepmom Leslie, Leslie's son Rob, and me—to erect the tepee, and I don't think it helped that the instruction book was thirty-one pages long, but when it was finally standing, it looked so inviting that Belle and Joe moved right in. Later, though, it started to get some excess slack and twisting in the canvas just below the smoke-flap hole. I consulted the instructions and read that, counter to what my intuition told me, the solution was to push the butt ends of the tepee poles out a few inches, and then go around the outside circumference of the tepee, yanking the canvas down lower on the poles, but when I followed these instructions it looked worse than before.

Then one day that summer Roy Reed came to visit. He'd driven up from Laramie to see his father Roy, still living in Jackson, and I invited them to drive over the mountains for lunch. Zelda had died a few years before but Roy Sr. was still going pretty strong, bowlegged and wiry in his cowboy boots at the age of ninety. I hadn't seen Roy Reed for decades, but he looked just like himself and he was still an Indian. His blond hair had gone white and it was grown to the middle of his back, tied with a thin strip of rawhide and the feather of a hawk. After we had lunch he took our tepee down and set it back up properly, not needing to consult the instruction book, not needing the help of another person.

Roy Reed was still making authentic Indian accoutrements, and he let Belle and Joe throw a couple of his spears until they got to where they could stick them in the ground where they wanted. Then he let them try on his buffalo headdress, which he'd made with the hollowed-out head and neck of a real buffalo. It came down well over Belle and Joe's shoulders and made them so top-heavy they had a hard time keeping their balance.

As I stood on the dirt of Wyoming with Roy Reed and the severed head of an animal with horns, it was almost like slipping through a wormhole in my mind. I couldn't help it; my thoughts skipped back to the day three small children and a teenage Indian tried to skin a dead bull and took its head off instead. I could've told myself at that moment that I'd actually managed, after everything, to circle all the way around. But by then I finally had a clear-enough view of the Pig Farm—what it was, and what it wasn't—and also of my own childhood, that I wouldn't have believed it.

I could never get a good look at my own upbringing, apparently, until I saw it from across a great chasm, a more than thirty-year span. I remember how I used to think, despite the way it caught me up at times, that the way our family tried to make a living raising cattle didn't pay off. The way it looks from where I am now, I can see that it was paying off the whole time, and I wish I'd told Mary something along those lines, or something bordering on gratitude.

I know that's why I felt so sorry for myself, so wretched, so bitter, when my mother died. There were some things I ought to have said to her. I never acknowledged the hundred years of hard exertion on the part of those who went before me, including her. I never said that I got it about the ranch, or about her, and I didn't even get it about myself, how lucky I was. Maybe I was waiting for her to tell me all about it—to explain how fantastic it all was—while she surely must have thought, knowing Mary, that I could figure it out for myself.

Although I was born and raised in Wyoming I think I had only one foot there the whole time. To my sorrow I have only one foot in Wyoming now. But I do understand after living for many years in the city that the land we had in Wyoming was an end in itself, the land and the animals and all the work that went with them.

Granddad, too, isn't with us anymore. He lived to the age of ninety-seven, and when he died was the country's oldest living former US senator. He'd outlived his daughter by more than thirteen years, and he'd made the most of them. He and Grammy had both weathered the loss of their daughter remarkably well. Although their hearts were broken, their advantage over me was that they didn't feel so sorry for themselves, not even at the beginning. In fact, a few weeks after Mary's accident, Brad told me that as they'd walked back to the hospital parking lot after learning that Mary was already dead when she'd arrived in the ambulance, Granddad said, "Well, we're all mortal."

Despite his shock and grief he couldn't help being fundamentally fair-minded. At the time I didn't look at it that way; my mother was not supposed to have been killed in a cattle drive, of all things. In my view the world had taken a very egregious wrong turn, so it took me longer to get back on my feet than it seemed to have taken Granddad and Grammy.

Of course, they also didn't have to come to terms with their own ingratitude, because there hadn't been any on their part. It was gratitude, in fact, that compelled Granddad to call me the year before he died to ask if I knew of a writer, one who lived, he thought, over in Alta or maybe in Driggs. I didn't know exactly how to answer that question. It could have been that he wanted me to do some writing for him but was reluctant to ask outright. He'd been known to call up my brother Brad to ask for a reference on a lawyer when he was really hoping Brad would take the job himself. And there was the slight possibility that he was truly confused—that he knew there was a writer in the vicinity but couldn't quite put his finger on the fact that it was his own granddaughter. Granddad was ninety-six years old, and his powers of recall weren't always perfect.

So I said, "No, I'm not sure I know any writers who live over in Alta or Driggs. Why do you need one?"

"I need someone to write my father's obituary," he answered.

Again, I wasn't sure how to interpret this, because although Granddad's mind was still mostly intact, I knew he'd called up Brad within the previous year, quite upset, to tell him, "My mother died," even though her life had ended thirty years before. So I tried to keep the conversation in the middle of the road.

"Why do you want his obituary written now, Granddad?" I asked. "He died in 1952."

"I know that," said Granddad. If my recitation of that fact made him impatient he didn't let it show in his voice. "But there was never a good memorial service, and there was never an obituary published in the paper."

And then Granddad told me, once again, the story of how his father had died rather suddenly while his mother was out of town, so they'd had only the briefest service during which, according to Granddad, "his name was barely mentioned." The worst part—and the part Granddad was most bothered by as his own life neared its end—was what their neighbor had to say as they left the church. Granddad had known and respected this man, his father's peer, all his life. "Why didn't you say something about your dad?" the rancher had asked.

I winced to hear Granddad tell that story again, knowing he was being too hard on himself, but I didn't think there was anything I could say to make my grandfather feel better about the moment that apparently haunted him. I didn't think he wanted consolation from me anyway. What he wanted from me—or from a writer who lived over in Alta or Driggs, who just might happen to be me—was help in writing his father's obituary and getting it in the paper. When he looked back at his own life, he felt so very thankful, and he was compelled to have history recorded, credit given, and the facts written down for others before it was all lost and forgotten.

That, I could understand.

So I sat down with Granddad on several occasions and heard him tell about his father's life, and because they were intertwined, his mother's life and his own life. He found for me the autobiographies, such as they were, of his mother and father. The obituary was written and submitted to the newspaper. The paper still hasn't published the death notice of a man who left us more than half a century ago, but Granddad seemed satisfied that at least the facts had been recorded by someone, and the burden seemed to have been lifted. When he died, he didn't seem to be troubled by anything except reluctance to leave my grandmother.

After Granddad's death I was watching some old interviews and news clips about him. He was asked by an off-screen reporter how he would like to be remembered. The interview had been mostly about politics, and I'm sure the reporter expected an answer that fit into that category. But Granddad replied to the question this way: "I hope they'll say that we took good care of the land."

I don't know about the idea of closure, whether there's any way to shut the books on an episode of your life, but for some reason last summer on our way back from a weekend at the Bar Double R, I pulled off the highway and drove slowly up the lane known as Mormon Row in Granddad's pickup, heading north up Antelope Flats. I had my daughter Belle with me, and I was looking for the spot where my mother had met her end so many summers before. I'd driven by Mormon Row and its adjacent fields perhaps thirty times since she died, but I hadn't wanted to set foot on it. I just kept thinking I wanted more time to pass, but for some reason one day it had.

The location where Little Joe reared over backwards with Mary had been described to me in some detail. I knew it was not too far from the south end of the lane, that there was a dead tree nearby, and that she had been on the flat and not the slopes of the butte. So when Belle and I climbed over the broken-down buck fence and walked out into the sage-brush and I saw the dead tree I knew I was close enough.

I can report that I found nothing in the way of enlightenment, nothing in the way of either a lingering presence or any explanation. I wasn't able to say "Oh, I see," the way you could if you looked over the edge of a high balcony from which someone had fallen. It looked about the same as a thousand other pieces of earth in that broad plain of sagebrush and grass and ground. My eleven-year old daughter didn't say anything to me as we tromped across the field, and she just let me stand there when I got to my spot. I looked to the east of us, squinting up toward the haunted town of Kelly over the big pastures that are no longer in alfalfa. The government let them go back to native grasses and sagebrush years ago, and they've been grazed since then by buffalo and antelope. My family's not herding cattle up that road anymore, so we don't have to worry about a cow bloat-ing on green alfalfa.

Although I'd gone out there looking for a spot on the ground, I was struck more than anything with what I saw when I looked up, rather than down at the dirt. Blacktail Butte was standing just to my west feathered with pine trees, and the Teton Range pocked with snowfields telescoped out to the north. Straight east I could see a sliver of scar from the Kelly slide, and above that bits and pieces of the upper Gros Ven-tre's red hills more than ten miles away, with the gray hump of Sheep Mountain rising farther on the southeast horizon. And the sky flaring over my head stretched wide and taut from peak to peak. It was so rich and cloudless, like we were all floating under a big blue parachute. The ground underneath me was just something to stand on, and I wondered why I was so vain as to have expected, in all the years it took to work up the resolve to walk out there, anything from that location other than its beautiful and raw neutrality. I had no desire to mark it with a pile of rocks or any other such thing as I suppose I once had in the back of my mind. I almost laughed at the idea, at how small it would have been on that particular landscape.

I'm not someone who believes that everything happens for a reason, but that maybe most things happen by accident. And as I stood there I knew that chance alone had caused my mother to be in a certain spot at a certain moment. That some electron somewhere had taken an unpredictable quantum leap, and things went to hell in a handbasket. I should have known there would be no solace for me in walking on the land where my own mother died, but maybe I did know, because I waited until I was past needing solace to seek it out. In any case, the lack of consolation was starkly apparent that day as I stood on the open land, trying to imagine such a big life ending as two creatures landed hard in a pasture for no particular reason.

Then Belle and I saw a movement just to the west, a black-and-white thing bobbing in place, and she spoke up in a whisper, asking what it was. We were compelled to walk toward it, slowly and as silently as we could in the brush. As we got closer we saw it was a big old badger, looking not at us, downwind of him, but in the direction of a small coyote about fifty yards farther west. No doubt the badger could not see the coyote, but he'd gotten a whiff of predator and was dipping his nose in the wind, his back to us.

The coyote pup saw all three of us. He'd seen Belle and me before we saw him, and he was watching us with a careful curiosity, trotting and walking in a big circle. Belle and I watched him as he watched us, trotting and walking as though on a tether, keeping his fifty yards' range. The badger let us get within ten feet of him, and when our presence finally superseded that of the coyote, he didn't panic; instead he actually faced us and had the temerity to look perturbed. And then he slowly backed into his den, dismissively flipping dirt out at us as he went, finally hiding himself completely from us and from all other creatures.

I don't know what my mother would say about my taking my own daughter and walking around on the sagebrush flat, looking for the place where she died. I don't know what she would say about my getting distracted from that purpose by a circling coyote and a badger who let me walk nearly to his door. And I don't know what she would say about selling the irreplaceable Bar B C and replacing it, for my part, with a 125-acre pig farm in Alta, on the wrong side of the mountains. But Belle and

I watched the coyote finish his 360-degree tour of the pasture, and then we got in the truck and drove over Teton Pass and back to the Pig Farm. And I don't plan on going out again on the flat by Blacktail Butte to look for anything.

When I picture Antelope Flats in my mind now, my mother and her cattle are not there. I see a wide-headed badger with a stripe coming down his sharp face, and a coyote walking around me at a safe distance, as faithful to his circle as the hands of a clock, all of it under a sky so blue you couldn't shoot an arrow through it.

I can't get back things that are no longer of this world. I do know that. I can't make my mother's cakes with store-bought cream. Posy's milk is merely legend now and I don't know what happened to the separator. I didn't ever recover the meat grinder from among my mother's things. Mary is gone, and now Granddad and Grammy, too. The endless ranch of my childhood belongs to other people. So I can't go back, I understand that.

But there is, for all its shortcomings, the Pig Farm. It might be right up against the state line but it's still on the right side of it. It's in Wyoming. Belle and Joe probably won't ever look at it the same way I looked at the Lower Ranch, but they have discovered a few things in the summers we've spent there. They've found already that horses can make very good companions. And someday they might decide that cows, too, are agreeable creatures. And perhaps at some point in their lives it will strike my son and daughter that they're partial to long views and wide skies and uncomfortable with little, closed-in places.

And even if none of those things comes to pass, maybe someday they might read my words. And then I hope they will come to understand a little about how miraculous it was—the land and the life that came down from my great-grandparents, from my grandparents, from my mother and my father.

And now, in the best way I can manage it, from me.

AFTERWORD

WHEN P.C. HANSEN DIED IN 1952, THERE WAS ONLY THE BRIEFEST SERVICE which included no words to eulogize this great man or commemorate his remarkable life, nor was an obituary ever published in the newspaper. It was his son Clifford Hansen's wish that a proper tribute finally be made to the father he so admired, so before he died at the age of ninety-seven, Granddad asked me to help him write one. The following is what we settled on.

PETER CHRISTOFFERSON HANSEN OBITUARY

Born September 16, 1867 — Died November 26, 1952
Peter Christofferson Hansen was one of Jackson Hole's early pioneers and a prominent area rancher. When he died in 1952 his wife Sylvia Hansen was in Denver with their two oldest children, where she was undergoing surgery for medical problems of her own. Because of her absence there was only the briefest memorial service at the Episcopal Church in Jackson, with no mention of his life events or accomplishments, and no obituary was written. Everyone assumed those things would be done when Sylvia returned home, but they never were. Peter's oldest surviving child, Clifford Peter Hansen, who at the age of ninety-six is our country's oldest living former US senator, now offers this obituary on behalf of his family, in honor of his father, and for those who might be interested in a few stories about early Jackson ranching.

My father, Peter Christofferson Hansen, was born on September 16, 1867, in Soda Springs, Idaho. His Danish parents came to America as converts to the LDS Church. As with many other LDS or "Mormon" converts, the opportunity to come to America was the dominating influence in their decision to join the church. I don't believe he and my mother ever attended the LDS Church.

As a young man Peter C. Hansen, known as P.C., worked in lumber camps. During their business careers his parents owned both sheep and cattle. One year P.C. and his brother bought some cattle from their father when prices were high, and when it came time to sell them, the market had dropped and they could not get enough money to repay the loan to their father. P.C.'s brother had a family to support, and got a job. But P.C. kept the cattle and ran them for three years, wintering them on the Snake River bottoms near Fort Hall, Idaho. The only way to feed his cattle in the winter was to ride his horse endlessly in circles, breaking trail through the snow. The horse's hooves pulled the long tufts of slough grass up through to where the cows could get at it and survive. P.C. slept in a tepee and before retiring would prepare fuel so he could have a little heat as he was dressing the next morning. In any case, it took three years before he was able to finally sell the cows and "break even."

At the time P.C. thought he'd used up three years of his life with nothing to show for it. But the bank in the area was aware of the story, and the credit P.C. gained later enabled him to make significant real estate purchases that he otherwise could not have made. He homesteaded in Jackson just before the turn of the twentieth century, near what is now Teton Village.

At one point while still quite young he lost an eye. He was digging a grave for the little daughter of a neighbor. The ground was hard and they were going at it with picks when a rock chip flew up and hit P.C. just above his right brow. He bled profusely, but rather than quitting the job he dabbed the wound with the dirty handkerchief of the man with him. From that he contracted erysipelas, a condition that nearly cost him his life. Much later he was able to go to Chicago to be fitted with an artificial eye to wear.

He and my mother, Sylvia Irene Wood, of Blackfoot, Idaho, were married in Blackfoot at the home of Agnes Just Reed, an old family friend. To this union six children were born: Parthenia, Geraldine, Clifford, Helen, Ordeen, and Robert. Dad had already lost his eye by the time he was courting her. They married for love.

After they were first married in the early 1900s P.C. worked on the coffer dam at Jackson Lake that was installed to facilitate the construction of the Bureau of Reclamation dam that now contains Jackson Lake. Sylvia cooked at the dam site (which later became Moran) in a tent for the crew, and made some candy for all of them to mark the occasion of Christmas. She was pregnant at the time with their first child, Parthenia.

They worked on the coffer dam until the day after Christmas, and then returned to their homestead to pack up and spend the rest of the winter in Idaho. P.C. went into the forest and cut four bent trees that he made into runners. He fit the wagon wheels into these runners, thus converting the wagon to a sleigh, and they drove it over Teton Pass behind six head of horses.

Later P.C. acquired some property in what is now the National Elk Refuge, which we referred to as "the swamp." The slough grass was an important source of feed and late fall supplement. It posed problems, however, because the cattle would wade into the open water holes and drown. Dad and I would construct fences to keep them out of the water holes. Weaning the calves late in the fall was accomplished by driving them from the swamp over to the ranch in Spring Gulch. After separating the calves from their mothers, we ran them just as fast as we could until they were tired enough that we could keep them under control.

P.C. and Sylvia removed sagebrush from property in the area by pulling a piece of railroad rail attached to a heavy log. This mechanism uprooted the sagebrush and made grass-seeding easier. My older sisters, Parthenia and Geraldine, would pile up the uprooted brush and set fire to it.

P.C. probably crossed the Snake River on horseback more than any other person. When he was living at his original homestead on the west side of the river, he was also acquiring land on the east side, and he had to feed cattle on both sides all winter long. One time he was riding a colt when crossing the river, and when it went under he lost his seat in his saddle. He managed to hold onto the horse's tail and make it safely out of the icy water. At that point the horse got away and P.C. had to walk the remaining three miles home. But he said that once his clothes had frozen stiff he was able to keep warm inside of them. Eventually he decided to consolidate his holdings on the east side of the Snake.

Later, when my parents moved to Zenith (near what is now the Jackson Hole Golf & Tennis Club) and started buying property there, the D.W. Standard Bank of Blackfoot, Idaho, told my father, "Buy anything you want.

Write a check and we'll cover it." During the Depression times were tough, and many people were forced to sell out. Some of them came to P.C. to buy their property because they trusted him to be fair. As word got around, other neighbors in the Zenith area sold their homesteads to Dad.

There was a man named Ed Martin who owned property in Spring Gulch. When Ed and Mrs. Martin were told by Dr. Charles Huff in the mid-1930s that Mrs. Martin would be well advised to move to a lower altitude, they said they would sell their place in Spring Gulch. By then I was grown and married to my wife, Martha, and we were keenly interested in buying it with my father's help. The price was agreed upon. Another rancher said he would pay more, but Mr. Martin said he wouldn't consider it. He said, "When Pete Hansen tells you he'll do something, there is no man whose word means more." I realized then how valuable a man's word was; it was the reason we were able to get the Martin place, and I thought it was a great tribute to my father.

P.C. and Sylvia were very devoted to each other. I remember that Mother would always be thinking of things she might do to be helpful to him that would relieve him of some of the worry.

As a father I remember him as honest and straightforward. I don't remember him shirking from any work. Although as he and Mother had small children for many years, I do remember at one time that Mother was unable to wash the diapers. I don't remember if she was away or what, but anyway, Dad hung the dirty diapers on the branches of a willow that made it possible for the water in the spring to get them somewhat clean.

P.C. Hansen was one of the first Teton County commissioners, and was in on the formation of Teton County when it became separated from Lincoln County. When he was a county commissioner they had to transcribe all of the records from Lincoln County, from which Teton County was formed. He was one of the founders of Jackson State Bank, and later, he became a member of the Wyoming Legislature.

At the end of his life he and Mother were living in the house built by the Charters, which was standing on the Lower Ranch when Mother and Dad purchased the property from Major C. C. Moseley in 1947.

Peter Hansen died of cancer on November 26, 1952, in the hospital in Jackson.

Acknowledgments

Thank you to Laura Yorke, for sticking with me and with this book long past what would be dictated by any reasonable agent-author relationship. Thanks to my editor Erin Turner for seeing what was there through the clutter. Thanks to Mary Kay Lazarus for helping me find both intellectual and emotional clarity. Thanks to Ann Cannon, Terrell Dougan, Maryellyn Larcom, and my dear Julie Lewis, for reading and responding to this book when it was a stretch to call it one. Thanks to my uncle Peter Hansen for filling in some things (including why my mother didn't like chickens, it having been his and my mother's job to clean the chicken coop), and to him and Nan Reppen for their help with the maps. Thanks to my father Pete Mead for setting such a wonderful example, and for sharing so many good remembrances with me. Thanks to my brothers Brad and Matt for growing up with me, and endless belated gratitude to those who came before: P.C. and Sylvia, Grammy and Granddad, and my amazing mother, Mary. And last, my love and thanks to my husband, Michael, and to our children, Belle and Joe, for coming with me to the Pig Farm and to Wyoming.

About the Author

Muffy Mead-Ferro is the author of the best-selling *Confessions of a Slacker Mom* and *Confessions of a Slacker Wife*. She's been published in two essay anthologies, as well as *Child* magazine and the *New York Times,* and has been featured on *Oprah, Today,* and NPR's *Talk of the Nation,* and in publications such as *The Atlantic* and the *London Times*. She and her family reside in Salt Lake City during the school year and in Alta, Wyoming, during the summer.